LEARNING ACTIVITIES FOR INFANTS AND TODDLERS:

An Easy Guide for Everyday Use

Betsy Squibb with Sally J. Deitz

Illustrated by Jean Iker

Edited by Carolyn Rutsch

Childrens Resources International, Inc., a nonprofit organization located in Washington, D.C., promotes the implementation of sound educational practices developed in the United States while maintaining the cultural traditions of the participating countries.

The Soros Foundations/Open Society Institute is a network of foundations, programs, and institutions established and supported by philanthropist George Soros to foster the development of Open Societies around the world, particularly in the former communist countries of Central and Eastern Europe and the former Soviet Union. To this end, the Soros Foundation cooperated with Children's Resources International to develop and implement the project called Step by Step: A Program for Children and Families.

Children's Resources International, Inc.
5039 Connecticut Ave, NW, Suite One
Washington, DC 20008
202.363.9002 *phone*
202.363.9550 *fax*
E-Mail: info@crinter.com
www.childrensresources.org

FOREWORD

In 1994, the Open Society Institute, Soros Foundations, and Children's Resources International (CRI) formed a partnership to introduce child-centered teaching methods to the well-established education systems of Eastern and Central Europe and the countries of the former Soviet Union. Its aim was to support the development of democratic ideals and principles within young children.

Step by Step, the educational reform program that grew out of this partnership, encourages children in preschool and primary school to think critically, make effective choices, and respect individual differences. The program supports teachers in their efforts to individualize instruction based on children's interests, strengths, and needs, and to include children from minority and special needs populations. In the Step by Step Program, the teacher becomes a facilitator of learning rather than a provider of information. Most important, family involvement is encouraged in all aspects of the program.

In 1998, Step by Step expanded to include infant and toddler programs. The CRI publication, *Creating Child-Centered Programs for Infants and Toddlers*, describes how to bring a child-centered approach to programs serving infants and toddlers. It has been used in the United States and internationally to assist caregivers in developing safe, supportive, stimulating learning environments for young children.

While conducting Step by Step training with infant and toddler caregivers in Eastern Europe, the authors of this book, Betsy Squibb and Sally J. Deitz, discovered that many caregivers want more than just curriculum methods. They want to know what activities they can do to help infants and toddlers develop in all areas: physical, emotional, social, language, and intellectual. And, they want this information available in a handy, easy-to-use format. To answer this need, we have produced *Learning Activities for Infants and Toddlers: An Easy Guide for Everyday Use*.

Learning Activities for Infants and Toddlers includes more than 125 learning activities based on current theory and research in infant and toddler development. Dr. Squibb is a professor of early childhood education at the University of Maine at Farmington. Dr. Deitz is an early intervention and blindness specialist at Orbis International in New York City. Both have spent decades providing support to providers of early care and education in diverse cultures and geographic settings.

Together, this book and its companion, *Creating Child-Centered Programs for Infants and Toddlers*, provide a comprehensive foundation of both methods and activities for use with very young children. While intended for caregivers, these publications are equally useful and informative for parents as they experience this period of tremendous growth and development with their children.

Pam Coughlin
Children's Resources International

TABLE OF CONTENTS

Foreword iii

Table of Contents v

Acknowledgments xi

1.   Introduction to Infant and Toddler Learning 1
Purpose of This Book 3
How Infants and Toddlers Learn 4
How Different Age Groups Learn 6
How Caregivers Can Support Learning...8
How to Use This Book 19
Activity Matrix 22

2.   Birth to Eight Months: The Non-Mobile Infant 27
What Is the Birth to Eight-Month-Old Child Like? 29

Understanding Self
Look, It's Me! 30
Gentle Touches 32
What Is Me and What Is Not Me 34

Understanding Others
I Can Smile! 36
Listening to the World Around Me 38
Laughing and Giggling 40
Watching the World Around Me 42
People and Things 44
Telling You What I Need...46

Understanding the World
Favorite Things 48
I Make Things Happen! 50
Learning New Shapes 52
New Textures and Sensations 54
Banging and Hitting Things 56

Communicating with Others
Playing Social Games 58
Making Sounds 60

Moving Around and Making Things Work
Holding Up My Head 62
Moving Together 64
I Can Lift My Head! 66
Looking Around 68

3.   Eight to Eighteen Months: The Mobile Infant 73
What Is the Eight- to Eighteen-Old-Month Child Like? 73

Understanding Self
Finding Something New 74
My Feelings 76
Dancing with Scarves 78

Taking Care of Self
This Is the Way We Wash Our Hands 80
Dressing Book 82
Pouring Water 84

Understanding Others
Book About Me 86
Friendship Mural 88
Our Coloring Box 90

Understanding the World
I Can Find It 92
Building a Tower 94
Circle Shape Drop 96
Sorting Shapes 98
Nesting Cans 100

Communicating with Others
Bear's Visit 102
Making Animal Sounds 104
Bumblebee Sounds 106
Texture Book 108
Finding Objects 110
Puppet Games 112

Moving Around and Making Things Work
Push Toys 114
Pull Toys 116
Creeping and Crawling 118
Dumping and Filling 120

Rolling Balls 122
Throwing Balls 124
Clothespin Boxes 126

4.   Eighteen to Twenty-Four Months: The Toddler 129
What Is the Eighteen- to Twenty-Four-Month-Old Child Like? 131

Understanding Self
I Know My Name 132
Doing It Myself 134

Taking Care of Self
Cleaning Up 136
I Can Dress Myself 138

Understanding Others
Comforting Others 140
Give Me a Hug 142
Playing in a Small Group 144

Understanding the World
I Can Make That Sound 146
Different Textures 148
Painting Time 150
I Can Guess What That Is 152
I Need Your Help 154

Communicating with Others
Telling What I Want 156
Singing 158
I Know Names of Things 160
My First Sentences 162
Telling You How I Feel 164

Moving Around and Making Things Work
I Love to Climb Things 166
Moving All Over 168
Moving Through a Maze 170
Big Movements, Little Movements 172

5.   The Two-Year-Old 175
What Is the Two-Year-Old Like? 177

Understanding Self
A Picture of Many Faces 178
I Am Happy, Sad, Scared, and Mad 180

Taking Care of Self
Matching Socks...182
Dress Up 184
Washing Up 186
Using Tools 188

Understanding Others
Celebrating Holidays...190
Teddy Bear Picnic...192
Making Gifts 194
Train Friends 196
Toddler Slumber Party 198

Understanding the World
Making Playdough 200
Torn Paper Collage 202
Collecting Natural Treasures 204
Printing Circles...206
Birds in the Nest...208

Communicating with Others
Story Time 210
Binoculars 212
Toy Telephones 214
Taking a Trip 216

Moving Around and Making Things Work
Puzzles...218
Making Raindrops 220
Feeding Birds 222
Exercising 224
Bottle Bowling 226
Scrub Painting 228

6.   Using Themes with Toddlers and Twos 231
Planning with Themes: Toddlers and Two-Year-Olds 233
Sample Theme—BREAD 236
Sample Theme—BALLS 237
Balls and Tubes..238
Ball Game 240
Ball Song About Rolling 242
Ball Song About Throwing 244

Sample Theme—FARM ANIMALS 247
Animal Stick Puppets 248
Finding the Animals 250
Matching Animals 252
Making Our Farms 254

Sample Theme—POCKETS 257
Matching Pockets 258
What Is in My Pocket? 260
Pocket Dance 262

Sample Theme—WATER 265
Making Rain 266
Making Bubbles 268
Water Painting 270
Puddle Jumps 272

7.   Families and Communities 275
Involving Families and Communities 277
Who Is on the Picture Cube? 278
Making a Necklace for Mom 280
Taking Care of Baby 282
Homes 284

Sounds Around Grandfather's Home 286
Grandmother's Tale 288
Visit by a Family Musician 290
Going over the Mountain to Visit 292

Family Fabrics and Clothes 294
Family Songs and Dances 296
Celebration Cards 298

Riding on a Bus 300
Listening to My Neighborhood 302
Smells of My Neighborhood 304

Cooking Applesauce 306
My Doctor and My Nurse 308
Work Hats 310

References 313

Appendix A: Developmental Milestones of Children From Birth to Age 3 314

Appendix B: Suggested Equipment and Furniture for Infant and
               Toddler Classrooms 316

Appendix C: Suggested Play Materials and Toys for Infant and
               Toddler Classrooms 317

Appendix D: Checklist for Selecting Toys and Play Materials for Infant
               and Toddler Classrooms 319

Appendix E: Sample Developmental Goals Chart for Infants and Toddlers 320

ACKNOWLEDGEMENTS

George Soros' abiding dedication to open societies and his belief that even the youngest members of society can practice basic democratic freedoms is the motivation for the development of this book and others in the series, *Creating Child-Centered Classrooms*. His Open Society foundations have supported our efforts to share child-centered teaching and learning methods with preschool, primary school, and teacher preparation programs in 26 countries and regions around the world.

The staff at Children's Resources International are grateful to Liz Lorant and Sarah Klaus of the Open Society Institute-New York for providing the direction and resources to enable the Step by Step Program to grow and flourish.

The Step by Step program teams and the teachers implementing this program were the first to recognize the need to expand the program to infant and toddler caregivers. Their dedication to creating quality educational experiences for children and their families is quite humbling. Through their hard work, they are indeed changing the world and making it a more caring and nurturing place for all children.

This publication *Learning Activities for Infants and Toddlers: An Easy Guide for Everyday Use* came about as a result of contributions from many individuals. The authors, Betsy Squibb and Sally J. Deitz, provided their expertise in infant and toddler developmental theory and practice. They developed the many wonderful learning activities included in the book. Carolyn Rutsch listened to the needs expressed for such a publication and made it a reality using her energy, tenacity, and foresight. She guided the publication and worked closely with the authors to make the book readable, easy-to-use, and informative. Jean Iker enlivened the cover and text with her illustrations, taking great care to make the drawings as instructive as the text. Elisa Slattery edited the book; with her easy style and eagle eye, she improved the book's readability and found errors the rest of us missed.

The photographs in the book were contributed by Krista Clapp, Therese Khan, Josie Robins, John Ordway, Zoe Bennington, Peggi Redalen, Jamie duPont, Kate Walsh, Marion Rutsch, and Diane Charnov. In addition, the staff at the Rosemount Center and St. Patrick's Episcopal Day School very kindly allowed us to capture wonderful moments of their programs on camera. Cassie Marshall designed the page format and produced a document that is a pleasure to look at and read. The Crosby Group developed a cover design that captures the whimsy and promise of the early years.

Each of the staff at CRI made contributions to this publication. Michele Redalen, in particular, served as staff photographer, editor, and production assistant. Pam Coughlin, Julie Empson, and Ellen Daniels reviewed the book.

The Staff of Children's Resources International

Chapter One

Introduction to Infant and Toddler Learning

The Purpose of This Book

This book offers caregivers and parents strategies for supporting infant and toddler development based on the latest information available on how infants and toddlers grow and learn. We now know more than ever before about the connection between brain growth and learning in the early years. Recent research shows that an infant's brain is extremely active—more than twice as active as an adult's brain. While their brains are developing, children learn at an amazing rate. In just three years, infants and toddlers learn to walk and talk. They begin to understand feelings and discover how to play with others. These early years of life are extremely important because so much learning occurs during every moment of the day.

Adults are the most important teachers in a child's life during the infant and toddler years. During this time, all adults, especially parents and caregivers, influence what and how a child learns. Children at this age depend on adults for eating, sleeping, and dressing. They depend on adults to help them learn how the world works. They also depend on adults to organize the environment for their most important learning activity—play.

This book is filled with activities that can be used by the adults who care for infants and toddlers. The adults may be caregivers who spend part or all of their day with children in early childhood education programs or classrooms. Or, they may be parents and family members who are looking for activities to support their child's learning. The activities in this book support the child's development in all areas: physical, emotional, social, language, and intellectual. They may be used as part of a daily schedule or plan, or incorporated into typical daily routines, such as diapering and feeding. Each activity includes a list of materials, steps for preparation, and ideas for interaction between children and adults.

Adult guidance and love is essential for infant and toddler development. We hope that this book will provide adults with a repertoire of learning activities that will help the young children in their care grow to their full potential.

This chapter provides a brief introduction on how infants and toddlers learn, how different age groups learn, how caregivers can support learning, how to work closely with families, and how to use this book.

How Infants and Toddlers Learn

Introduction

Infants and toddlers are capable of complex and varied learning. In the first years, the child learns how to move around, communicate, make connections between experiences, understand feelings, and cooperate with others. Because learning at this age involves different interrelated areas of development, the child's learning process is quite complex. The caregiver needs to consider the connected nature of the young child's learning. For example, a nineteen-month-old child begins to use language. As she does this, she is developing a sense of herself as a speaker as well as developing pride in her speaking accomplishments. In this way, her social, emotional, and language capabilities are developing together.

The learning that an infant or toddler accomplishes is holistic because it involves all areas of the child's development: physical, emotional, social, language, and intellectual. These various areas change rapidly and often overlap as the child grows. The significance for the caregiver is that one activity might be effective for supporting multiple areas of development. For example, a five-month-old child who plays with a rattle is learning about what rattles do. The child is also discovering how to grasp and move the rattle. He is using his eyes and learning to look at an object while it moves. Adults need to plan activities for every area of development. (See Appendix A for a Chart of Development and Learning of Children from Birth to Age 3.)

Theories of Learning

Theories of how children learn help caregivers understand the complex nature of learning. They also provide a framework for interpreting the child's everyday behaviors. For example, a child who wants to pull off her own socks is beginning to become independent and develop a sense of self. If the caregiver can recognize the distinct patterns of learning that relate to the child's age group and developmental level, she can support the child's optimal level of accomplishment. The caregiver can use this new information and the theories of learning to plan the most appropriate activities for children. The following is an overview of research on brain development, temperament, and learning.

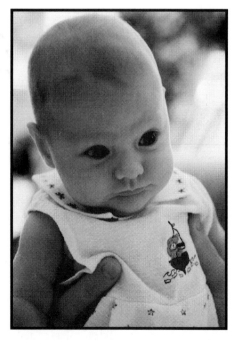

We know that when children are born, their brains are still growing and developing. In the first eight months of the child's life, the brain matures. Connections are made for "wiring" the brain. The child experiences the world and the brain makes patterns of these connections. For example, infant play involves repeated interactions and explorations. These repeated experiences make the brain connections permanent. Knowing the importance of this play for infants and toddlers will help adults carefully choose activities for children that support the brain's organization and development.

Theories of learning can also help guide adults in planning activities. For example, some theories tell us how children learn about the world and how they develop language. Other theories explain how children develop a sense of themselves and others.

Infants and toddlers learn through their senses. The child psychologist Jean Piaget labeled the first two years the *sensorimotor* stage. Children at this age use their senses and physical abilities to understand the world. They learn by moving objects and by examining their shapes. The child under two years of age repeats actions over and over in order to understand what is happening. Their early experiments with objects are important for solving problems later on.

An important development for infants in the first year is *object permanence*. In the first months, the child thinks an object exists because he can see it. If the adult hides a toy under a cloth, the child with no object permanence will not look for it because he believes the object no longer exists. Sometime after eight months, the child understands that the object exists even when it is invisible. The child searches under the cloth for the toy. Object permanence helps children adjust to separation from their parents. It also forms the foundation for later learning about symbols in reading and mathematics.

Other useful theories offer information about the connections between adults and child development. L.S. Vygotsky and other theorists of child development suggested that adults have a major role in structuring or *scaffolding* learning. This means the adult describes the child's play and makes a scaffold for it. The adult's description or scaffold helps the child understand and remember his play. The adult in this role is called a "mediator" of learning. Adults can also be "collaborators" in learning. A good example of this collaboration is an adult and a child reading a book together. Reading *with* a young child, not *to* the child, is a shared or collaborative experience. The adult and child talk about the book and share ideas. They can share the turning of pages. Collaborative reading experiences are pleasurable for the child and this type of shared experience helps children enjoy reading.

Another example of scaffolding can be seen when an adult helps a child learn about shapes using a shape sorter, a toy where the child places small shapes in holes of a same shape. The child may first pick up the shape and try pushing it into a hole of a different shape. The adult can assist the child by saying the name of the shape and then physically guiding the child's hand to match the shape with the correct hole. After the child is more comfortable with this activity, the adult may only say the name of the shape and let the child find the hole by himself. Eventually, the child will be able to complete the activity without the adult naming the shape or guiding the child's hand. In this way the adult has carefully structured the child's learning, leading him to independent completion of this activity and fostering his ability to recognize and say the names of shapes.

Other helpful theories include the development of *self*. Infants and toddlers learn that they are separate beings from others. M.S. Mahler and other theorists have described the process of learning about the self. By seven to nine months, infants begin to show us that they "recognize" themselves as separate. By age two, they discover they are separate beings from adults. Children need the love and comfort of attentive adults in order to develop as individual persons.

Caregivers can also benefit from theories about *temperament*. Children are born with different styles of behavior or temperaments. This temperament affects the child's particular style of learning. An example of how temperament differs among children is the approach of two children to a new toy. Tara is an easy-going child and Barbara is more cautious with new toys. Tara will rush to play with a new toy while Barbara refuses to touch it. To prevent Barbara from being upset, parents and caregivers need to offer new materials carefully. Barbara's caregiver could encourage her to watch other children play, and in this way give her lots of time to begin to play with new toys.

Theories on the development of the child's thinking and her perception of self can help caregivers understand children's behavior. For example, adults know that when an eight-month-old looks in a mirror it is a step towards the child understanding how to feed and dress herself. Theories can also be used to guide adult behavior with children. For example, we know from Vygotsky's theory that what the adult says and does influences the child's learning. For example, when a sixteen-month-old is struggling to pull a toy train with a string, adults can describe the process of pulling and the child  will understand and remember this situation when faced with new challenges. Understanding how children learn helps caregivers understand the particular child they are nurturing and to see their role as helpers in the child's development process.

How Different Age Groups Learn

Infants and toddlers are generally considered to be between the ages of birth to three years. Some people think of only two age groups: infants, who are up to one year, and toddlers, who are from one to two years. However, in this book, we use a definition that is functional, or based on what children with typical development can do. The functional definition includes four age groups: (1) birth to eight months, (2) eight to eighteen months, (3) eighteen to twenty-four months, and (4) two-year-olds. The infant in the first eight months moves only a little, so he is called non-mobile. The mobile infant is from eight to eighteen months of age. This child is moving, and will progress from crawling to walking. The third group is toddlers, who are eighteen to twenty-four months old. The two-year-old, ages twenty-four to thirty-six months, is the fourth group. In this book, activities are presented separately for the toddler and two-year-old. Separating the activities for these two groups makes it easier to find the most appropriate activity for each age group. Two-year-olds are often capable of using some of the same materials as older children, although they do this in different ways.

The Young Infant (0 - 8 months)
Learning for young infants is very different from that of older infants and toddlers. Infants depend on adults to bring experiences to them. In particular:

- They learn to feel comfortable with adults and prefer learning in the company of familiar adults.
- They learn to trust adults as they are being fed, held, and dressed.
- They sleep often and learning occurs when they are awake or *alert*.
- They learn by looking and listening.
- They touch and grasp objects as they learn about them.
- They put things in their mouth to explore them.

The Mobile Infant (8 - 18 months)
The mobile infant is experiencing major changes, including learning her first word and taking her first step. Mobile infants learn best from loving interactions with adults. In particular:

- They know the difference between familiar and unfamiliar adults and prefer learning in the comfort of familiar adults.
- They copy adults.
- They learn language from adults. (The mobile infant understands a lot of language but speaks only a little.)
- They move and make choices among playthings.
- They actively explore objects.
- They learn by playing with the same toy again and again, but changing their actions slightly each time.
- They spend less time in the routines of dressing, sleeping, and eating, and more time playing.
- They are social and watch others carefully.
- They learn by playing simple games with one caregiver. Gradually, they can play simple cooperative games with two or three children.

The Toddler (18 - 24 months)

Toddlers are different types of learners. They are explorers and investigate language, ideas, and people. They are learning about being a separate person and they do this by watching and playing with others. In particular:

- They have lots of conflicts with other children about toys. These conflicts are valuable for learning about self and others.
- They are learning about different emotions. They do this through observing their own feelings and those of others.
- They engage in parallel play with peers—they will play at the same activity side by side.
- They are beginning to talk. They progress from two words to simple conversations.
- They are constantly discovering things and how they work. They use all of their senses as they explore objects.
- They delight adults with their beginning pretend or imaginary play.
- They have less obvious physical development than the mobile infant. They are working on moving smoothly and balancing.
- They are fascinated by their developing independence, such as learning how to pour juice and dress themselves. Their movements are clumsy and they often knock things over and spill liquids.

The Two-Year-Old (24 - 36 months)

Two-year-olds are both similar and different from toddlers. Like toddlers, two-year-olds are busy discovering. However, two-year-olds are more independent. Their play is more organized and can last longer. In particular:

- They play with what interests them at the moment. Their play at an activity can be very quick.
- They do not do well with lengthy planned activities. The time spent playing in a single activity varies from 10 seconds to 10 minutes or more.
- They learn through warm personal contact with adults.
- They play without adults.
- They play alone and with peers. They frequently engage in parallel play and small groups of two or three form naturally as they choose activities.
- They learn through simple themes that are connected to their life, such as animals, water, and balls.

How Caregivers Can Support Learning

Caregivers of infants, toddlers, and two-year-olds have an important job. What children learn at this age provides the foundation for later schooling. Caregivers must understand what each age group is like and how those children learn best. It is the adult's job to plan activities that match the individual temperament and the interests of the child. Caregivers can plan for the individual child using a variety of different approaches, including: (1) interacting with children, (2) choosing toys and materials, (3) organizing toys and materials in the classroom, (4) arranging the space or environment, (5) developing the daily schedule or routines, and (6) working closely with parents.

Interacting with Children

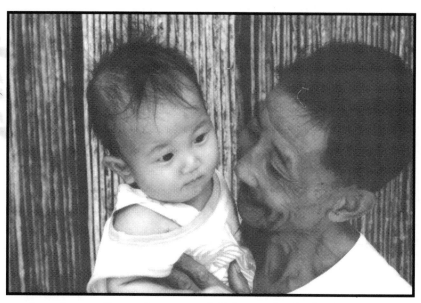

Talking and playing with adults is the major way infants and toddlers learn. While it is valuable for children to learn to play independently, they will learn more if they spend time with a supportive adult. Caregivers of infants and toddlers should place themselves near the children. For example, the caregiver can sit on the floor, hold the child on her lap, or kneel to work at the same level as the child. When working with a group, the caregiver might have one or two children very close by and another two children a little farther away.

Caregivers interact with infants and toddlers by talking with them. Adults use a special form of speech called "parentese" with the young infant. They talk slowly and exaggerate the sounds. As the infant begins to make sounds, the adult repeats these. Adults vary their voices when they speak with infants and, as a result, children learn high and low pitch.

The mobile infant is just beginning to say words. At this stage, adults talk about the child's play. Some ways that adults verbally support mobile infants include:

- Describing children's actions and choices ("You picked up the ball.")
- Repeating children's words ("Yes, you are drinking more juice.")
- Simplifying children's phrases ("Ball goes down the slide." Or "We eat.")
- Referring children to each other for peer talk ("Anna is eating.")
- Talking with and encouraging children who are not yet speaking

Language for two-year-olds includes all of the above and more. For example, adults use more complex phrases to describe the child's play. They engage in two-way conversations and make suggestions as two-year-olds play. Caregiver language encourages children's understanding of words as well as of their actions.

Adults also use nonverbal methods for teaching infants and toddlers. Nonverbal support is important for children in all four age groups. For the young infant, careful observation is the key. The adult watches the child's behavior for clues on how the child is learning. It is important for the adult to first observe if the child is alert and calm. When a child is relaxed, it is easier for her to focus and learn. More nonverbal clues to what the young infant is saying during play are listed below.

Infant Behavior	What Behavior Means	Caregiver Response
Face-to-face, gazing at adult	Interested in playing or interacting	Talk with infant, present an object, or begin a game
Face-to-face, smiling	Interested and pleased	Continue with play
Head turned slightly away	Interested, but needs adult to change play	Play more slowly or faster
Glances away	Losing interest	Vary the play, add something new, talk about what the child is looking at
Turning head rapidly side to side	Dislikes something	Try a new object or game
Head lowered	Not interested or wants to be left alone	Stop. The child has had too much stimulation
Cries, splays fingers, arches back	Distressed, unhappy, sick, uncomfortable	Stop and comfort the child with soothing words and gentle touches

Caregivers can use these behaviors as guides to assist them in observing infant behavior for calm, alert times. An infant who is stressed or feels over-stimulated will send signals to a familiar caregiver.

For the child over eight months, adult nonverbal support includes:

- Observing the child's play to understand the child's abilities
- Showing interest in the child's play
- Being near and available to help
- Listening to and accepting children's words and explanations of their play.

Choosing Toys and Equipment

Adults support learning by choosing the right toy at the right time. The caregiver tries to understand the child's interest and level of ability. Other guidelines for choosing toys for a group of children follow.

- Toys and equipment need to be safe. Pull cords on toys should be less than 32 cm long and all play items should be wider than the opening of a 35 mm film canister or toilet paper roll.
- There should be sufficient toys and materials for sharing. Having two similar toys is a good idea, since infants and toddlers are too young to understand sharing. It is easy to offer a similar toy (for example, a second pull toy) to a waiting child. It is very difficult for children to wait to share.
- There should be enough toys, but not too many. Bring out a few toys at a time.
- Adding different types of toys offers the child new learning experiences.
- Infants and toddlers like to play with ordinary things. Familiar objects from home are interesting. All age groups love to play with wooden spoons and metal or plastic bowls. For pretend play, toddlers and twos enjoy using used baby clothes for dressing dolls and old pans for pretend cooking. They will dress up in scarves, hats, and old clothes. Toddlers will make music with pots and pans, wooden spoons, bowls, and simple bells.

Appendices B and C offer suggestions for equipment, furniture, and toys for infant and toddler classrooms. Appendix D is a short checklist for the caregiver to use in selecting safe and appropriate toys and play materials.

Organizing Toys and Materials in the Classroom

Adults can support learning through the arrangement of toys and materials. The following are a few guidelines for displaying toys and arranging centers or play areas for infants and toddlers. More information on toy and material selection can be found in Appendix C, Suggested Play Materials and Toys for Infant and Toddler Classrooms.

The Non-Mobile Infant (0-8 months) Organizing toys for the young infant is different from organizing for older children. Two easy methods are to (1) organize by *developmental level*—for example, shelves or bins of toys are grouped for infants from birth to four months and four through eight months, and (2) organize by *similar actions*—for example, group toys that use the same skills together on shelves or in bins. Some examples of toys with similar actions are stacking toys, nesting toys, musical toys, soft toys, noise makers, teethers, visual toys such as mirrors, and toys that roll such as balls.

Mobile Infants and Toddlers (8-24 months) The display of toys for mobile infants and toddlers is important for promoting individual choice. Setting shelves at the child's level helps a child make her own choices. These two age groups want to do things independently. The caregiver will need to limit the amount of toys mobile infants and toddlers have at one time. Having just a few toys makes it easy to find things. The caregiver can place similar toys together, which helps children learn to organize their play.

Two-year-olds (24-36 months) The placement of toys on low shelves is important for two-year-olds. They can help with clean-up when the shelves are simply organized and easy to reach. Two-year-olds still need some duplicate or similar toys. If the shelving is a neutral tone, children can see the colorful toys more easily.

Picture displays can also add to learning. The child will touch and pull at the pictures, so it is a good idea to cover them with clear covers. Caregivers can make displays of things children like. For example, caregivers can collect pictures of different types of dogs or trains, and place them at the child's eye-level.

Caregivers can also make simple games for two-year-olds. Matching games are popular and can be made with pictures or with items from home such as socks or mittens.

The Arrangement of Space

There is more than one way to arrange the classroom for learning. One of the biggest challenges for all age groups is finding enough space for (1) the routines of eating, sleeping, dressing, and washing, and (2) playing. One solution is to use the same area for more than one activity. Caregivers can move cribs into one part of the room and change sleeping space into play space. They can also use the same table for both playing and eating.

Adults may want to vary the classroom for different age groups. The young infant rooms offer safe, nurturing care. There are cribs, a rocking chair, and a low table for the infant to pull himself up to a standing position, pillows and cushions for sitting and climbing, and a rug for crawling on.

The eight- to eighteen-month-olds like to practice moving. Equipment such as a slide or large soft cushions to climb can be placed in the center or corner of the classroom. When organizing play space for children at this age include three or four activity areas or centers. These centers include:

- space for sensory play—sand, water, simple art
- quiet book and language area
- simple pretend play corner
- center for manipulative toys and simple blocks (Manipulative toys engage the child in using his hands to explore and construct. Examples include simple puzzles and building blocks.)

Materials will move with the children from center to center—this is normal. For example, children use pull toys all over the room. They will play with light blocks and these are easy to move; children place them in wagons and haul them.

Space for children over eighteen months is different from space for younger children. These areas or centers need more specialization. The best room arrangements have simple basic learning centers, more similar to those for three- to five-year-olds. The shelves and furniture are smaller than those for children over three years. One example of this is a toddler-sized sensory table where children can play with sand, water, or other sensory materials. Sensory tables, also referred to as sand and water tables, have one or more basins on a low table where up to six children can play. Centers for toddlers and two-year-olds include the following:

- sensory area (includes a water and sand table and small easel)
- simple pretend play space (includes items to act out family roles)
- books in a cozy area
- blocks and vehicles
- music
- manipulatives and simple puzzles
- large movement or motor area for dancing, group time, or indoor vehicles.

Toddlers and two-year-olds work alone or in small groups. The centers do not need to be large. Caregivers can place similar activities together or near each other. For example, manipulative toys and books are quiet activities and can be near each other. A small table or an easel for art, and a sensory table for sand and water might be located together. Place these next to the sink to simplify cleaning for children. Large group activities are brief for this age group and usually occur in the large movement or play area.

Adults can support learning in the room arrangement by considering these guidelines for different age groups. Caregivers working with children of mixed ages face a challenge when trying to arrange the room for everyone. A secluded area, with dividers to keep older children outside, is a good idea for non-mobile infants. Place their books and manipulatives inside along with cushions and mats for lying on.

Room Arrangement for Non-Mobile Infants

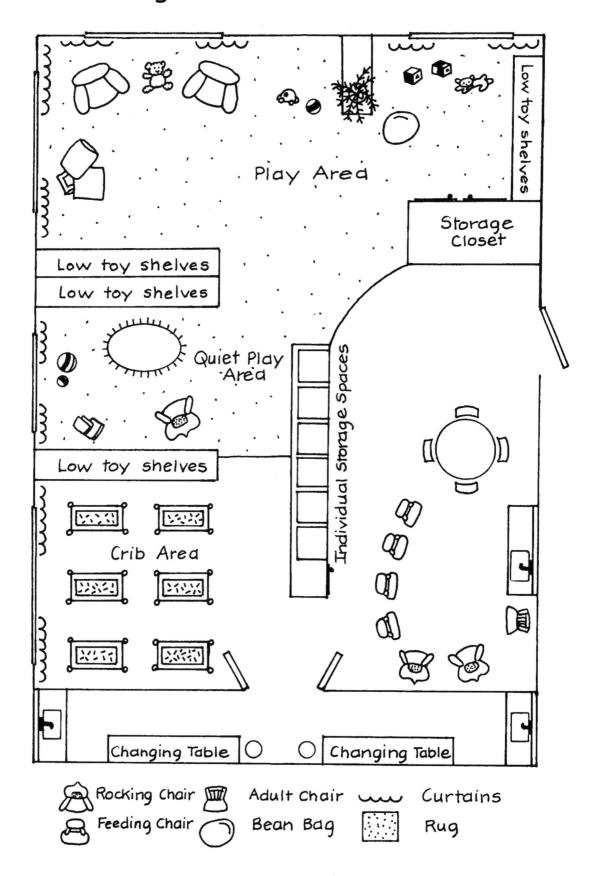

Play Area

Low toy shelves

Low toy shelves
Low toy shelves

Quiet Play Area

Low toy shelves

Crib Area

Individual Storage Spaces

Storage Closet

Changing Table ○ ○ Changing Table

Rocking Chair   Adult Chair   Curtains

Feeding Chair   Bean Bag   Rug

Room Arrangement for Mobile Infants

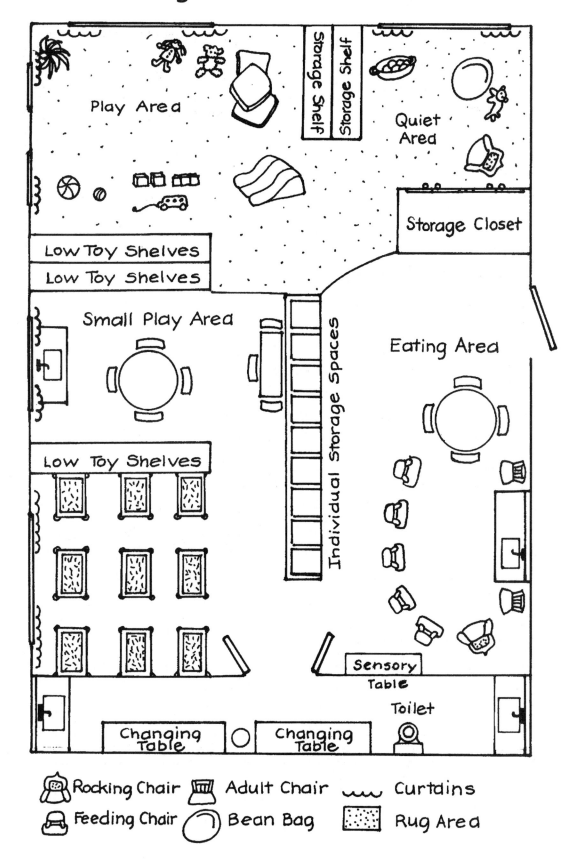

Play Area

Storage Shelf

Storage Shelf

Quiet Area

Storage Closet

Low Toy Shelves

Low Toy Shelves

Small Play Area

Individual Storage Spaces

Eating Area

Low Toy Shelves

Sensory Table

Toilet

Changing Table

Changing Table

Rocking Chair   Adult Chair   Curtains

Feeding Chair   Bean Bag   Rug Area

Outdoor Play Area

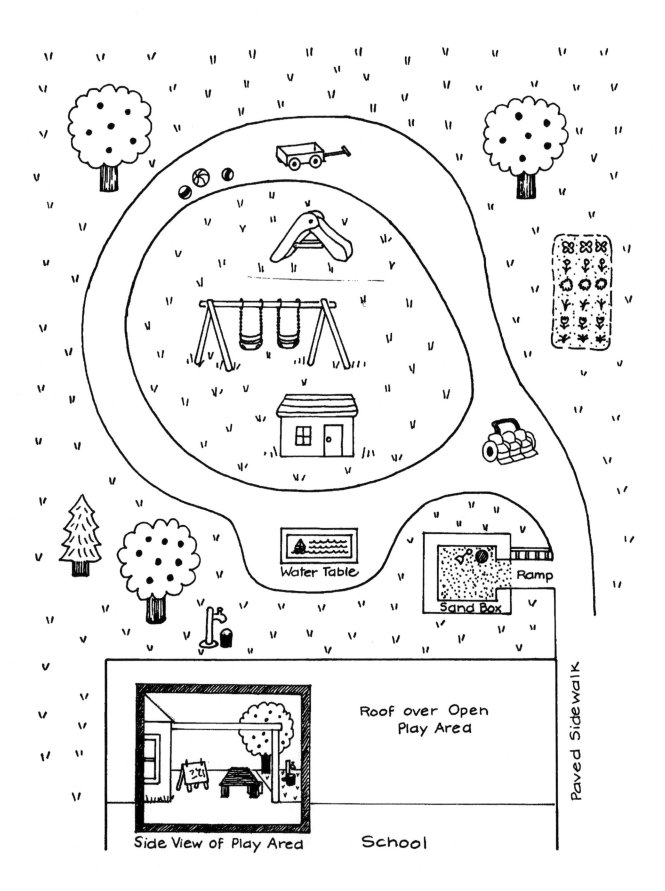

Water Table

Ramp

Sand Box

Roof over Open Play Area

Paved Sidewalk

Side View of Play Area

School

All of the age groups like familiar, stable arrangements. They feel comfortable when they can find their favorite toys. Remember to make major changes in the room arrangement only once in a while. Small changes will make the room interesting; big changes may frustrate the children.

Planning the Day

A lot of the young child's time is spent eating sleeping, dressing, diapering, and washing. Adults can take advantage of these routine activities to support learning. One way to do this is to add language to these routines. For example, the caregiver explains to the child what she is doing and what the child is doing. This provides the child with a scaffold for the experience. Another way is to turn a routine into a learning activity and let the child help. For example, the child can hold the diaper while the caregiver is undressing her.

The daily schedule includes routines of arrival and feeding. Here are some examples of different learning for young infants, mobile infants, and toddlers during these activities:

Daily Routine

Routine	*Non-Mobile Infant*	*Mobile Infant*	*Toddler*	*Two-Year-Old*
Arrival	• smiles • reaches • coos, babbles	• waves "hello" • vocalizes • begins to take off outer clothes	• says "hello" • walks steadily • helps take off outer clothes	• says "hello" to adults/peers • walks carrying bag • takes off clothes • puts coat away
	• cries/fusses to indicate hunger • makes eye contact • smiles, vocalizes • reaches, holds bottle	• points/gestures to indicate need • eats finger food • begin to use utensils	• says she is hungry • climbs into chair • eats independently • indicates "more" • indicates "finished" • washes and dries hands	• asks "what's for dinner?" • sits near peer • pours milk • labels food • says "finished" • cleans hands

More examples can be found in Appendix E, Sample Developmental Goals Chart for Infants and Toddlers.

Routines also involve small groups. Mealtimes, dressing to go outside, and leaving the room are all natural group times. Caregivers can make these routines into fun learning experiences.

Singing songs and doing finger plays offer toddlers a focus for the activities. Adults can make up songs about the activity.

Young children can learn about taking care of play materials when they help clean up. Toddlers love to help, and they can assist in the clean-up at the end of a play period. The older infant can pick up and put toys in a bucket. Older toddlers can help adults pick up toys and put them on a shelf.

A consistent daily schedule is important for young children. The youngest infants will each have an individual schedule. Mobile infants, toddlers, and two-year-olds are able to have a more uniform schedule where everyone eats, sleeps, and plays at the same time. A schedule for children this age includes time for play alone or with peers, play indoors and outdoors, and time for routines. Play times of one hour or more are best for learning. All age groups enjoy a regular schedule because they learn to anticipate what activity is next, and this gives children a sense of security.

The planned curriculum for infants and toddlers is different from that of older children. Infant and toddler curricula involve planning for daily interactions with materials, the caregivers, and one another. The caregiver focuses on *how* the child relates to the materials and people and not *what* the child makes. Many activities in this book describe planning daily activities using materials found in the classroom.

Most caregivers of young children plan one daily activity that is different from the usual offerings at play time. The children are free to choose this activity, watch, or play somewhere else in the room. This activity is teacher-initiated and needs more adult supervision than some of the other choices. Some examples of these activities are included in this book. These include the activities, "New Textures and Sensations" in Chapter 2, "Making Animal Sounds" in Chapter 3, and "Printing Circles" in Chapter 5.

Working Closely with Parents

Caregivers can support children's learning by working closely with their parents. Parents are a child's first and most important teachers and have the greatest influence on their child's development. Consequently, a partnership between parents and caregivers is best for each child's healthy development. Caregivers can share what they did in the classroom and parents can repeat these activities at home. Parents can describe the child's favorite toys and activities and caregivers can continue these activities in the classroom. This type of sharing offers the child a chance to repeat actions and strengthens her understanding.

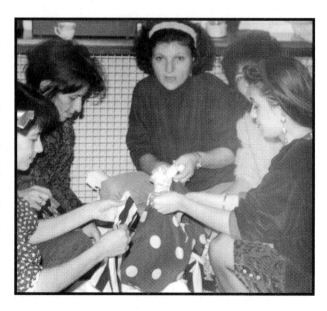

Families can be involved in the classrooms in many other ways. They can assist in the classroom and serve as decision-makers on parent advisory committees. Working parents may have limited time for helping in the classroom and attending meetings. The following are some of the ways busy parents can contribute:

- Parents can help supply teaching materials. Caregivers can give parents a materials list which might include items such as used pots for pretend play or pieces of fabric to make into baby blankets. The list can be posted on the bulletin board or printed in the newsletter.
- Parents can offer songs and stories. Family members often have favorite songs or stories to share with the classroom.

How to Use This Book

This book includes numerous learning activities that caregivers can use with infants and toddlers. These learning activities include the routines of dressing and napping and playing with materials. The activities are organized into seven chapters. Chapter One is this Introduction. Chapters Two through Five feature a wide range of learning activities that are grouped for the four infant and toddler age groups. Chapter Six suggests a method of planning learning activities for toddlers and two-year-olds using themes. Chapter Seven includes activities designed to involve families in the classroom. Together, these activities and methods offer a range of experiences to support learning in all areas of a child's development.

Activity Format

Each activity includes a purpose, suggested materials, directions for preparation, activity directions, suggestions for how to extend or vary the activity, and a home connection. The "Purpose" of the activity clarifies what the activity is and its intent. The directions indicate how to prepare the activity and the necessary materials to carry it out. Each activity includes recommended ages, which means that most children of that age will be appropriately challenged. Ideas for varying the activity are included under "Extensions and Variations." This section includes suggestions for modifying the activity to suit both younger and older children. Caregivers working with mixed-aged groups will find this section helpful. Finally, there are ideas for involving parents and other family members in the activity titled "Home Connection."

Symbols

Illustrated symbols quickly identify the activity's main audience and developmental goal or goals. All activities are designed for children ages birth to three years. However, each activity has a symbol in the upper left hand corner indicating the activity's specific, intended age group. For example:

Each activity also includes picture symbols which identify the areas of development that the activity will support. These picture symbols are located on the upper right hand corner of the activity. Caregivers can use the picture symbols to select activities that promote different areas of development. Each picture symbol represents a different area of development. The symbols and titles for areas of development are as follows. Activities to promote emotional development are included under the titles "Understanding Self" and "Taking Care of Self." Activities to promote social development can be found under the title "Understanding Others." Intellectual development is under "Understanding the World," language development is under "Communicating with Others," and Physical development is under "Moving Around and Making Things Work." The following picture symbols are used to represent the different areas of development for the child:

 Understanding Self (emotional development)

 Taking Care of Self (emotional development)

 Understanding Others (social development)

 Understanding the World (intellectual development)

 Communicating with Others (language development)

 Moving Around and Making Things Work (physical development)

The Matrix

The matrix at the end of this chapter is a guide for choosing activities for the different areas of development. This matrix includes all of the activities in the book, arranged so that caregivers can select particular activities to promote different areas of development. For example, to choose an activity that fosters language development in a toddler, the caregiver looks under "Communicating with Others" in the matrix. Some activities are good choices for more than one area of learning. When appropriate, the matrix also identifies the second or third area of learning or development that the activity promotes.

Chart of Development and Learning

The Chart of Development and Learning of Children from Birth to Age 3 helps caregivers identify at what ages children typically can do different tasks. (See Appendix A.) The chart also lists the abilities of most children at a certain age. For example, if a caregiver wants information on what types of things toddlers can do physically, she looks for physical development of toddlers on the chart. This information gives ideas on what activities might be appropriate to challenge the child. For example, toddlers can learn to kick a ball. Consequently, the adult knows to prepare an activity in which a small group of children practice kicking.

The chart presents information on how children grow in a typical pattern. Some children may lag behind in one area. A small delay in one area is not worrisome. Delays in several areas are a sign to the adults to observe the child carefully. If delays continue over time, educational specialists may want to further assess how best to teach the child. Caregivers can use the chart to check a child's progress and to plan appropriate learning activities.

Activity	Age in Months						Page Number
CHAPTER 2							
Look, It's Me!	3-5.5	X					30
Gentle Touches	0-6	X					32
What Is Me and What Is Not Me	0-6	X		X			34
I Can Smile	1-5.5		X		X		36
Listening to the World Around Me	0-6		X	X			38
Laughing and Giggling	1-6		X				40
Watching the World Around Me	0-3		X				42
People and Things	2-6		X	X			44
Telling You What I Need	0-3		X				46
Favorite Things	1-3			X			48
I Make Things Happen!	3-6			X			50
Learning New Shapes	3-6			X			52
New Textures	2-6			X			54
Banging and Hitting	6-9	X		X			56
Playing Social Games	2-6		X		X		58
Making Sounds	0-2.5		X		X		60
Holding Up My Head	2-4					X	62
Moving Together	0-6					X	64
I Can Lift My Head!	3-5					X	66
Looking Around	0-3					X	68
CHAPTER 3							
Finding Something New	8-10	X					74
My Feelings	13-18	X					76
Dancing with Scarves	13-18	X				X	78
This is the Way We Wash Our Hands	10-18	X			X		80
Dressing Book	8-18	X			X		82
Pouring Water	13-18	X				X	84
Book About Me	8-12	X	X				86
Friendship Mural	13-18		X			X	88
Our Coloring Box	13-18		X	X			90
I Can Find It	8-10			X			92
Building a Tower	10-12			X		X	94
Circle Shape Drop	10-18			X		X	96
Sorting Shapes	16-18			X			98
Nesting Cans	10-18			X		X	100

22

Activity	Age in Months						Page Number
Bear's Visit	8-12				X		102
Making Animal Sounds	10-12			X	X		104
Bumblebee Sounds	13-18				X		106
Texture Book	13-18			X	X		108
Finding Objects	13-18			X	X		110
Puppet Games	10-18				X		112
Push Toys	8-10					X	114
Pull Toys	10-18					X	116
Creeping and Crawling	8-18			X		X	118
Dumping and Filling	10-18	X				X	120
Rolling Balls	8-12		X			X	122
Throwing Balls	13-18					X	124
Clothespin Boxes	16-18					X	126

CHAPTER 4

Activity	Age in Months						Page Number
I Know My Name	18-24	X					132
Doing It Myself	18-24	X					134
Cleaning Up	18-24	X					136
I Can Dress Myself	18-24	X				X	138
Comforting Others	22-24	X	X				140
Give Me a Hug	18-20	X	X				142
Playing in a Small Group	18-24		X				144
I Can Make That Sound	18-21			X	X		146
Different Textures	18-24			X		X	148
Painting Time	18-24			X			150
I Can Guess What That Is	18-24			X			152
I Need Your Help	18-24		X	X			154
Telling What I Want	14-20				X		156
Singing	18-23				X		158
I Know Names of Things	19-24			X	X		160
My First Sentences	18-24				X		162
Telling You How I Feel	18-24	X			X		164
I Love to Climb Things	18-24		X			X	166
Moving All Over	18-24					X	168
Moving Through a Maze	18-24			X		X	170
Big Movements, Little Movements	16-24					X	172

Activity	Age in Months						Page Number
CHAPTER 5							
A Picture of Many Faces	24-36	X				X	178
I Am Happy, Sad, Scared, and Mad	24-36	X					180
Matching Socks	24-36	X		X			182
Dress Up	24-36	X		X			184
Washing Up	24-36	X				X	186
Using Tools	24-36	X				X	188
Celebrating Holidays	24-36		X				190
Teddy Bear Picnic	24-36		X				192
Making Gifts	24-36		X	X		X	194
Train Friends	24-36		X			X	196
Toddler Slumber Party	24-36		X	X			198
Making Playdough	18-36			X			200
Torn Paper Collage	24-36			X	X		202
Collecting Treasures	24-36			X		X	204
Printing Circles	24-36			X		X	206
Birds in the Nest	18-36			X		X	208
Story Time	18-36		X		X		210
Binoculars	24-36			X	X		212
Toy Telephones	24-36		X		X		214
Taking a Trip	24-36			X	X		216
Puzzles	18-36	X		X		X	218
Making Raindrops	24-36			X		X	220
Feeding Birds	18-36			X		X	222
Exercising	18-36	X				X	224
Bottle Bowling	24-36		X			X	226
Scrub Painting	24-36			X		X	228
CHAPTER 6							
Balls and Tubes	18-36			X			238
Ball Game	18-36		X			X	240
Ball Song About Rolling	18-36			X	X	X	242
Ball Song About Throwing	18-36			X	X	X	244
Animal Stick Puppets	18-36			X	X		248
Finding the Animals	18-36			X		X	250
Matching Animals	24-36			X	X		252
Making Our Farms	24-36		X	X			254

Activity	Age in Months						Page Number
Matching Pockets	24-36			X		X	258
What Is in My Pocket?	24-36			X	X		260
Pocket Dance	24-36					X	262
Making Rain	18-36			X			266
Making Bubbles	18-36			X			268
Water Painting	24-36			X		X	270
Puddle Jumps	24-36			X		X	272

CHAPTER 7

Activity	Age in Months						Page Number
Who Is on the Picture Cube?	6-36	X	X		X		278
Making a Necklace for Mom	18-36		X			X	280
Taking Care of Baby	8-36		X	X			282
Homes	8-36	X	X				284
Sounds Around Grandfather's Home	8-36		X	X	X		286
Grandmother's Tale	8-36		X	X	X		288
Visit by Family Musician	12-36		X		X		290
Going over Mountain to Visit	18-36		X	X		X	292
Family Fabrics and Clothes	18-36		X	X			294
Family Songs and Dances	0-36		X		X	X	296
Celebration Cards	18-36		X		X	X	298
Riding on a Bus	15-36			X		X	300
Listening to My Neighborhood	8-36			X	X		302
Smells of My Neighborhood	12-36			X			304
Cooking Applesauce	18-36			X		X	306
My Doctor and My Nurse	18-36	X		X			308
Work Hats	12-36			X			310

Chapter Two

Birth to Eight Months:
The Non-Mobile Infant

What Is the Birth to Eight-Month-Old Child Like?

The child at this age is beginning to understand the daily rhythms of her world and the people in it. She will learn to trust the people around her through various frequent events such as bathing, being held, being dressed, and eating/nursing. Although she will sleep frequently, a lot of learning will occur when she is awake and alert. She is learning how to communicate with others through simple vocalizations and cries. The birth to eight-month-old will enjoy being held and moved gently in the caregiver's arms, as well as exploring her own fingers and toes. She will show interest in the colors, sounds, and people around her. A child at this age loves touching and grasping objects and exploring them with her mouth.

Here are a few major characteristics of the birth to eight-month old:

- Begins to have some head control and learns to hold her head up
- Enjoys being held and rocked or moving rhythmically with a caregiver
- Prefers to learn while comfortable with a familiar adult
- Begins to recognize herself in a mirror
- Learns to smile at familiar people and things
- Engages the caregiver and indicates wants and needs in simple ways
- Enjoys learning by looking and listening to things as they are happening around her
- Begins to laugh and giggle
- Touches and grasps objects such as rattles and soft toys
- Explores things by putting them in her mouth
- Engages in simple interactive play with the hands and fingers of caregivers.

When planning classroom space for infants of this age, make sure the room has soft areas with pillows and soft surfaces in which the child can roll over, prop himself up on his elbows while lying on his stomach, sit alone without support, and lie on his stomach or back with assurance of safety. The activities in this chapter are for individual infants, as children this age do not play in groups. If there are older, active children in the same classroom, plan a space apart from them for these young babies. Babies this age will enjoy simple finger games with a caregiver, small rattles, small shiny or soft toys/objects, and making noise with household objects. They enjoy being held and rocked by a caregiver, particularly to music. Although at this age they prefer to play alone with a caregiver rather than with other children, they will tolerate being near other children as they play. They will begin to make sounds and use their voice to communicate. Plan to have space and time to interact, hold, cuddle, and play with babies of this age.

Look, It's Me!

Purpose: The child will approach his own image in a mirror and show interest in it, such as staring at the image, reaching or crawling towards it, or patting the mirror. At this stage in the child's life, he may not realize that the reflected image is his own, but he will still enjoy looking at himself and the caregiver in the mirror.

Materials: small mirror or shiny metal baking pan (if the reflected image in the pan is clear)

Preparation:
1. In selecting the mirror for this activity, make sure that the mirror is small enough to be held, will not shatter if broken, and has rounded rather than sharp edges.
2. Hold the child on your lap so you are both facing the mirror.

Activity: Tap on the mirror to draw child's attention to it, then smile and point to child's reflection. Point to the reflection and say the child's name, or make a silly face that the child likes you to make. Assist the child in touching the image in the mirror. Say things like "Look at the baby!" or "There you are! That is Stephen!"

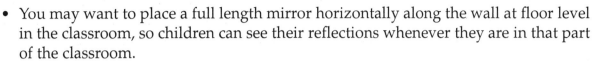

Extensions and Variations:

- You may want to place a full length mirror horizontally along the wall at floor level in the classroom, so children can see their reflections whenever they are in that part of the classroom.
- Include small mirrors among the toys you offer children while they are lying on the floor or in their cribs.
- To ensure safety, you may want to cover mirrors with clear contact paper.
- You may also place a large mirror flat on the floor and place the child on top of it, encouraging the child to crawl along it and see his reflection.
- When outdoors with the child, do this activity with shiny, reflective surfaces or with water, such as a pond or puddle.
- This activity can be done with 2 or 3 children playing on the floor with a large mirror on one wall.

HOME CONNECTION

Encourage families to play with children at home using mirrors that will not break or shiny cooking pans. Brothers and sisters may enjoy doing this activity with the child while meals are being prepared, or in the bath.

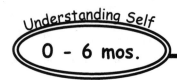

Gentle Touches

Purpose: The child develops a sense of trust through touching and being touched. This teaches the child that she can trust her environment, that she is cared for when she needs to be, and that she will be soothed when she is distressed.

Materials: none

Preparation: Hold the child or be near the child.

Activity: Hold the child close, providing support and moving her gently and calmly. Softly touch the child's head, cheeks, arms, legs, fingers, and toes. Hold the child's hand and rub it gently against your cheek. Speak to the child soothingly while you pat her back and gently rub her arms and legs.

Extensions and Variations:

- During baths, gently massage the child with your hand or with a soft cloth.
- Following the bath, gently rub oil or lotion on your hands and rub the child's back, feet, arms, legs, hands, and fingers.
- If child is happy, content, and relaxed, he will be soothed and sleepy as you do this.
- You can do this activity as often as you find time throughout the day.
- Try this activity outside on a sunny day. You can sit on the grass with the child lying on a soft blanket or towel.
- Many parents enjoy being in a group with their children at this age, sitting in a circle and giving their children gentle massages while the parents talk to each other.
- If parents come to your school or class to pick up children at the end of the day, or if they arrive at the same time in the morning, a parent-child massage group may provide a calming transition for both parents and their children.

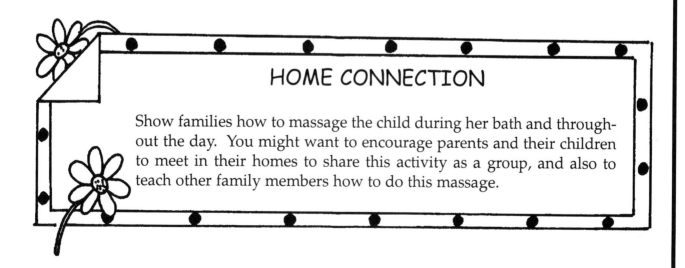

HOME CONNECTION

Show families how to massage the child during her bath and throughout the day. You might want to encourage parents and their children to meet in their homes to share this activity as a group, and also to teach other family members how to do this massage.

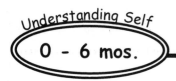

What Is Me and What Is Not Me

Purpose: The child learns to feel the difference between himself and other objects. The child begins to learn where his body begins and ends, and that other objects are separate from him. This activity is one of the earliest processes of the child defining himself, and seeing himself as a person separate from other people and things in the world.

Materials: child's book, rattle, soft toy, wooden block, or other safe objects

Preparation: Hold the child or be near the child while he is in the bath, crib, or on the floor.

Activity: Gently stroke the back of the child's hand and then place an object such as a rattle in his hand. Touch various body parts and say their names, such as "Here are your toes!" or "Look at your big foot!" Touch and gently stroke the child with various objects, such as a soft toy, rattle, ball, soft cloth, small book, or wooden block. You may want to rub the child's hands or feet together, or place his hand on one of the objects such as the ball.

Extensions and Variations:

- This activity can be done before and after the bath when the child has no clothes on. This will let the child enjoy the feeling of the crib, towel, or blanket all over his body.
- Try this with the child on his stomach and on his back.
- This activity can be done on a walk outdoors. The caregiver can help the child feel leaves, flowers, bark of trees, grass, a park bench, or garden soil.
- In each season, the child can feel seasonal outdoor weather, such as snow, rain, summer sun, or wind.

HOME CONNECTION

Encourage families to continue exposure to these various textures in the home. Some of the child's favorite textures and objects may go back and forth from school to home in order to have continuity in this activity.

I Can Smile!

Purpose: The child smiles, gazes intensely, and interacts with the caregiver when approached socially.

Materials: none

Preparation: Select a time when the child is alert and content, not when she is crying or uncomfortable.

Activity: Hold the child facing you, or have the child lying down in front of you, and speak to her with animation and eye contact. Stay close to the child and gaze into her eyes. Smile at the child, make silly sounds, or "walk" your fingers up and down the child's arms while you are talking. Say things softly such as "There you are!" or "Who is this cute child?" or "Are you having fun with me?"

Extensions and Variations:

- Do this activity for short intervals throughout the day, such as during diapering, bathing, waking from a nap, dressing, and feeding.
- Play simple games in which you alternately clap your hands and the child's hands, while talking softly to her.

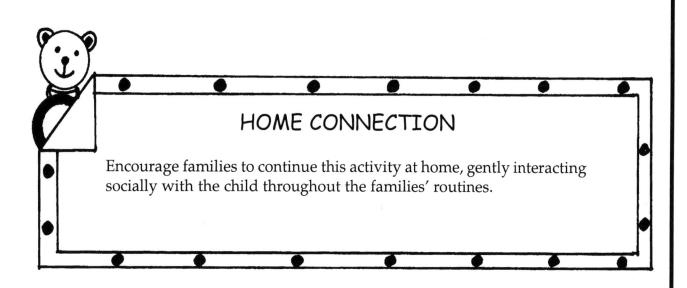

HOME CONNECTION

Encourage families to continue this activity at home, gently interacting socially with the child throughout the families' routines.

Listening to the World Around Me

Purpose: The child learns to listen to the caregiver's voice and other familiar sounds from the environment.

Materials: none

Preparation: Hold the child or be very close to the child.

Activity: Talk to the child in soft, calm, soothing tones. Stand behind child and say "Can you find me? Try to find me. Where am I?" Encourage the child to turn her head, smile, or respond to your voice in any way. Whisper softly in the child's ear, then in the other, nuzzling and saying endearments. Encourage the child to respond through movement, smiling, laughing, or vocalizing.

Extensions and Variations:

- Shake a rattle or other noisy object gently to see if the child responds.
- When outdoors with the child, mention sounds in the environment such as a bus, an airplane, a car, thunder, or greetings from friends or neighbors.
- Try this activity in a circle with a few other children and parents. Have all parents make the same noise or sing the same song.

HOME CONNECTION

Show families how to do these activities using noise-producing objects at home, and encourage them to carry out these activities at home and outside as well. Some sounds will be found at home that are not at school, and the child may enjoy these. These may include a ticking clock or the sound of a family pet.

Laughing and Giggling

Purpose: The child laughs as he learns to communicate with the caregiver about what he enjoys around him. When the child feels pleasure, joy, and happiness, his laughter tells the caregiver which interactions and activities are his favorites.

Materials: none

Preparation: Do this during any activities throughout the day when the child is alert and happy.

Activity: Play interactively with the child to encourage laughter. Do playful things such as tickling the child's stomach, gently bouncing the child on your knees, or playing "Pat-a-Cake" (clapping your hands alternately with child's hands). Stop from time to time to observe the child and watch for his responses to these activities.

> *Pat a cake, pat a cake, baker's man,*
> *Bake me a cake as fast as you can,*
> *Pat and roll it and mark it with a "T"*
> *Put it in the oven for Thomas and me.*

(The "T" refers to the first letter of the child's name.)

Extensions and Variations:

- Have conversations with the child using different playful voices, such as high-pitched tones and silly facial expressions.
- Observe the child's reactions to see what he thinks is funny.
- He may like silly, repetitive singing, spontaneous games of "peek-a-boo" (in which you hide your face behind your hands and surprise the child by opening your hands), or gentle tickling.
- This activity can be done with a small group of up to 3 children, playing a game of tickling, playing "peek-a-boo," or singing songs.
- With a small group of up to 3 babies, this activity allows you to notice their different reactions and observe temperament styles.

HOME CONNECTION

Encourage families to watch for events throughout the child's day that make the child laugh. Demonstrate for the family the activities at the program that make the child laugh and chuckle. Ask the family what things they do at home that cause the child to express happiness.

Watching the World Around Me

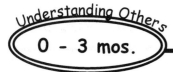

Purpose: The child begins to look at the caregiver's face and at other familiar objects. During this time in a child's life, she is learning about the world around her by looking, focusing, and gazing at familiar people and things. It is valuable to provide interesting things for the child to see.

Materials: simple toys such as rattles, pictures of faces, soft toys, large plastic rings, or any other brightly colored objects

Preparation: This activity can be done while holding the child in the caregiver's lap or on the floor, crib, bath, changing table, or child's soft chair.

Activity: Holding your face or a colorful object about 6 to 15 inches in front of the child's eyes, encourage the child's eye contact. Talk to her and change your facial expressions playfully. Move the object slowly around the child's field of vision.

Hang a piece of thick string across the child's crib and tie on ribbons, soft toys, familiar objects, and bells. These items can be changed every few days to keep the child's interest. As the child grows, she will reach out and hit the objects. Be sure to supervise this activity at all times and to discontinue this after the age of 6 months, or whenever the child begins to sit up in her crib.

You may also place hanging mobiles near the child's crib, and colorful pictures on the walls at the child's level.

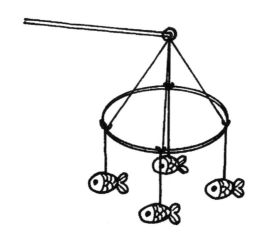

Extensions and Variations:

- Place colorful things around edges of the crib, the room, and the child's outdoor area.
- Children enjoy objects that have bright colors, simple designs, highly contrasting colors, geometric shapes, and faces.
- Make a mobile to hang near the child's crib or bath.
- When playing outdoors with the child, or when taking a walk, point out the bright colors and shapes you see. For example, you might want to show the child the brightly colored fruit, vegetables, cartons, or other containers at a local market.
- Show the child objects that appear in nature, such as flowers or bright leaves.

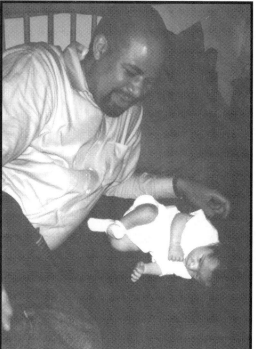

HOME CONNECTION

Show families how to do these activities, and teach them to make the mobiles and crib bands. In a parent meeting, have parents make mobiles and crib bands.

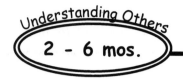

People and Things

Purpose: The child interacts with familiar people and objects and begins to conceptualize the difference between persons and things.

Materials: familiar toy or hand puppet

Preparation: None; this activity can be done at any time that the child is quiet and receptive.

Activity: Hide behind a door, chair, or crib. Say "Where am I? See if you can find me." Then come out and say, "Here I am!" You may also want to try using a hand puppet, playfully having a conversation with the child. Talk directly to the puppet, then have the puppet "talk" to the child, have the puppet "talk" to you, and watch the child's reactions. Place the child's hands on your face and hands, then place them on a toy. Talk about each thing the child touches.

Assist the child with exploring a toy, then in exploring your face and hands.

Extensions and Variations:

- As the child explores a new object or toy, describe it and show the child how to use it.
- If the toy is too advanced for the child to use alone, demonstrate the toy and show how it works.
- Exaggerate your delight in this toy and in its colors, sounds, form, and movement.

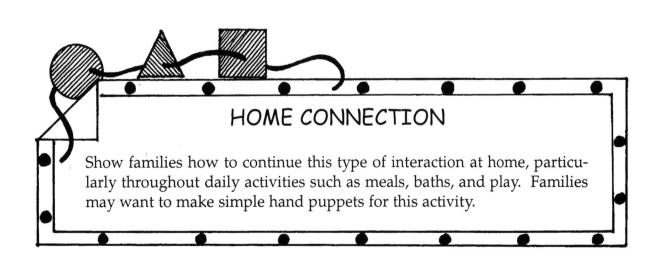

HOME CONNECTION

Show families how to continue this type of interaction at home, particularly throughout daily activities such as meals, baths, and play. Families may want to make simple hand puppets for this activity.

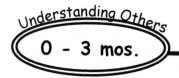
Telling You What I Need

Purpose: The child learns to communicate needs to the caregiver and learns that the caregiver responds quickly to the child's needs. These needs include thirst, hunger, feeling tired, and being uncomfortable for any reason.

Materials: none

Preparation: None; this activity can be done throughout the day whenever the child signals his need for attention from the caregiver.

Activity: If the child cries, respond immediately and try to find out whether he is hot, cold, wet, bored, ill, or soiled. While you do this, talk to the child soothingly. Pick him up and hold him, rock him, speak soothingly, and assure him of your presence. As the child calms down and looks at you, continue eye contact and reassurance. Any time the child initiates his interaction with you, either by looking at you or moving his arms and legs, pick him up or talk to him to assure him of your presence and your willingness to communicate with him. If the child becomes fussy by averting his gaze or splaying his fingers, calm him by leaving him alone and allow him time to calm down.

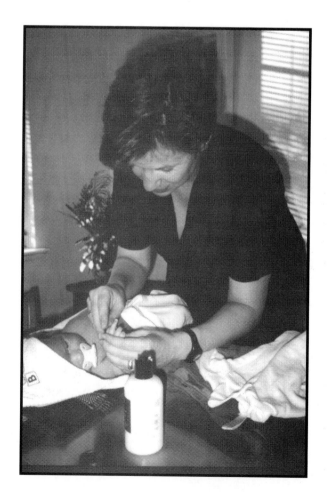

Extensions and Variations:

• This activity becomes a consistent response of caregivers when the child signals that he needs attention.

• Ideally, each caregiver in the child's environment will learn how to interpret the child's signals so that his needs are met in a timely manner.

• Signals of a child's desire to communicate with a caregiver often occur at meal times, bath times, as a child wakes up from sleep, and at playtime.

HOME CONNECTION

Help families to interpret the child's signals, and to respond consistently. Assure families that responding to the child's signals for communication does not spoil the child, but gives him a sense of safety and security that will increase throughout childhood.

Favorite Things

Purpose: The child becomes emotionally attached to familiar objects, toys, photographs, and pictures. These emotional attachments provide the child with a sense of security, comfort, and familiarity. When some familiar objects are removed and replaced later, they seem new to the child. This way the child has objects around her which are both familiar and new.

Materials: familiar objects, toys, pictures, and photographs that are safe and do not hinder child's movements

Preparation: Child may be lying in crib, on caregiver's lap, or on floor on clean towel, blanket, or cloth.

Activity: Place familiar pictures, toys, and objects in child's crib. Change soft toys, stuffed animals, pictures, and photographs from time to time so that there are always some new and some familiar things for child to explore. Suspend a toy over the crib, changing the toy to a picture with a design, a photograph, or a brightly colored object to continue child's interest.

Extensions and Variations:

- Encourage the child to hit and bat the toy that is dangling above the crib.
- Occasionally place a toy above the crib that will make a noise when the child hits it, such as a rattle.

HOME CONNECTION

Ask families about the child's familiar objects or favorite toys at home. Arrange for some favorite, familiar objects to go home and back to the program with the child. Some favorite home objects may also be brought to the program for child. Encourage the family to play with the child using familiar objects and toys.

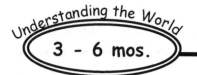
I Make Things Happen!

Purpose: The child begins to understand that his actions and movements produce changes, resulting in some new event.

Materials: rattle, rolling toy, or any other safe object

Preparation: The child may be in any position, held, sitting, in bath, or eating.

Activity: Help the child tap a rattle suspended above him. Show him how to kick or bat a small ball across the floor or crib. Place a small bell on a bracelet around the child's wrist or ankle so that it makes a noise when he moves.

Extensions and Variations:

- During bath time, the child might make noise with plastic objects while playing in the water.
- At mealtimes, the child might make noises by hitting his spoon on the table or tapping his cup against the plate.
- Try this activity with 2 or 3 babies sitting in a circle supported by caregivers. Assist them with rolling a soft ball from one to another.
- A simple rattle can be made from a small balloon, can, or plastic container sealed with a few beans placed in it.

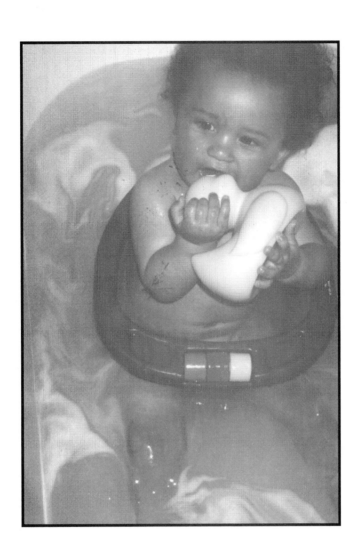

HOME CONNECTION

Encourage families to observe the child's efforts to make noises or other effects by acting upon objects. Show families the ways in which the child does this at school. Explain that this is the way the child learns how to associate his actions with results, which is the beginning of learning about objects in the world around him.

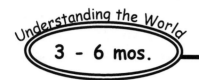

Learning New Shapes

Purpose: The child learns about shapes and forms by touching and holding objects.

Materials: variety of round, square, triangular, conical, and tubular objects—may include balls, a paper roll, a square block, a rubber ring, or plastic cups

Make sure that these items are large enough so that the child will not choke on them (larger than a film canister or small pill bottle, but small enough so that the child can grasp them).

Preparation: This activity may be done at any time the child is relaxed and alert.

Activity: Offer a range of objects of varying shapes to the child and encourage her to hold each one. Vary the selection and talk about the differences in shape and feeling of each one. Encourage the child to explore her fingers and toes when she is not wearing shoes. Paste shapes of different textures and materials on a paper. These may include pieces of carpet, cotton balls, soft cloth, sponge, felt, wool, sandpaper, or fur. Show the child how to explore these varying textures and shapes.

Extensions and Variations:

• Whenever you take the child on a walk outdoors, collect various shapes and textures such as sticks, leaves, stones, flowers, and plants.
• Fill a box with objects of various shapes for the child to play with.
• This box can include rattles, plastic spoons, balls of yarn, balls, and blocks.

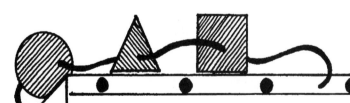

HOME CONNECTION

Show families how to play with the child using these shapes and items. Caution them to ensure the child's safety regarding the size of the objects. Some common household objects are useful for this activity, such as empty paper rolls, lightweight plastic kitchen utensils, and simple non-breakable objects.

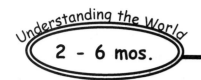

New Textures and Sensations

Purpose: The child touches different things to learn about varying textures. The child begins to explore the various properties of objects and how they feel to the touch. Learning to feel different sensations of touch is a precursor to the child's future understanding of different materials in his environment.

Materials: various textured materials such as fur, towels, feathers, silk, leather, wool, lace, embroidery, cotton, and burlap.

Preparation: This activity can be done any time that the child is alert and ready to learn.

Activity: Gently stroke the child's legs, stomach, face, arms, and back with materials of these varying textures. Give the child balls made from materials of varying textures, such as toweling, cotton, wool, and satin. Use words to describe the textures, such as hard or soft or rough.

Extensions and Variations:

- Sew a cover or quilt made of squares of cloth of varying textures and colors.
- This cloth can be placed on the floor with the child on top of it to encourage exploring the feelings of the different cloths.
- When you are outdoors with the child, assist him in exploring the textures around him, such as the tree bark, the smooth leaves, the prickly grass, the hard rocks, or the soft flower petals.

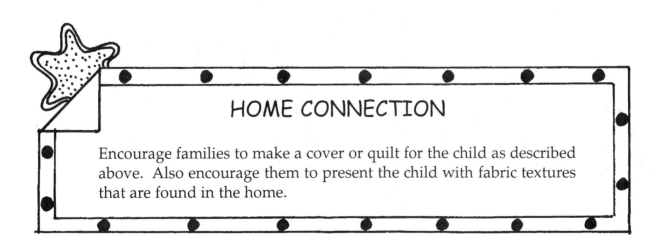

HOME CONNECTION

Encourage families to make a cover or quilt for the child as described above. Also encourage them to present the child with fabric textures that are found in the home.

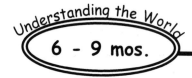

Banging and Hitting Things

Purpose: The child learns about objects that are fun to bang, hit, and pat. This activity assists the child with learning about the properties of things in the world through the senses of touch, sight, and hearing.

Materials: wooden spoons, lids, pots, pans, rattles, or plastic balls

Preparation: This activity can be done at any time, holding the child in caregiver's lap, playing on the floor, or at a table.

Activity: Holding the child on your lap, encourage her to hit the tabletop with her hand, a spoon, or a toy. Give her objects that are noisy when banged, such as wooden spoons and lids or pots. Show the child how to make noise by banging these objects, patting other objects such as a ball, and batting hanging rattles.

Extensions and Variations:

- Encourage the child to pat a wide range of common objects with her hands, including furniture in the classroom.
- Talk to her about the different sounds she hears and the different sensations she feels.

HOME CONNECTION

Encourage the child to pat objects of varying sizes and shapes. Encourage her to pat other children and pets gently. Also show the child how to pat other household items such as blankets, soft toys, and furniture.

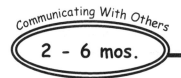
Playing Social Games

Purpose: The child enjoys social play and fun interaction with a caregiver, making silly sounds and faces. This activity is a foundation for future learning and social relationships. The child learns that she can respond to the actions and sounds of the caregiver and that the caregiver will respond to the child's sounds and movements. These activities are the beginning of the child learning to create an effect in the world around her.

Materials: none

Preparation: Select a relaxed time when the child is alert and active.

Activity: Make a silly sound such as a click and wait for the child to copy you, dance to music while holding the child, or tickle the child lightly on the cheek when you notice her watching you. Listen to hear if the child makes a silly sound, then copy it. You may also rhythmically pat the child's feet or hands, play "peek-a-boo" by dropping a light soft cloth over the child's head and encouraging her to pull it off, or copy a movement she makes.

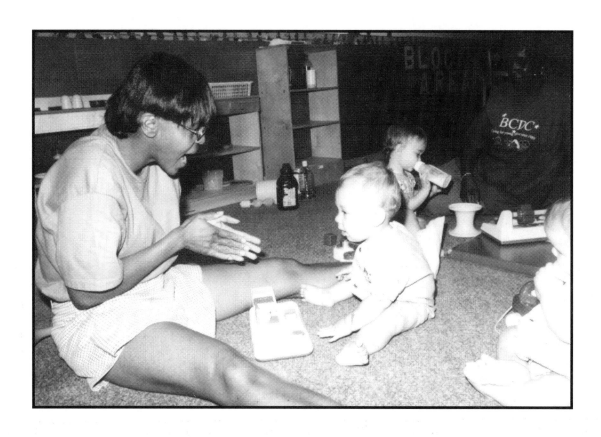

Extensions and Variations:

- These social interactions may be done during dressing, bathing, feeding, and at other times throughout the day.
- Games may include songs about the fingers and toes while playing with these, making a movement in response to the child's movement or sound (such as nuzzling the stomach each time the child laughs, or kissing the hands or fingers each time the child vocalizes), and responding to subtle efforts on the child's part to communicate through eye contact, sounds, or movements.

HOME CONNECTION

Suggest that families initiate fun interactions with the child by being playful and observing when the child appears to want interaction. Family members can imitate the child's movements and sounds and encourage the child to imitate their simple sounds and silly facial expressions.

Making Sounds

Purpose: The child makes his first sounds. A child's first sounds are soft vocalizations he makes when he feels comfortable. These sounds happen naturally and are not made on purpose. The muscles in the throat, which are used to make these sounds, will later be used when the child talks.

Materials: none

Preparation: Hold the child facing you or have the child lying on a surface in front of you, facing you.

Activity: Listen for random sounds such as "aaah" or soft cooing noises. When you hear a sound, smile at the child, talk to the child, or imitate the sound the child made. Do this throughout the day while dressing, changing diapers, bathing, or playing with the child.

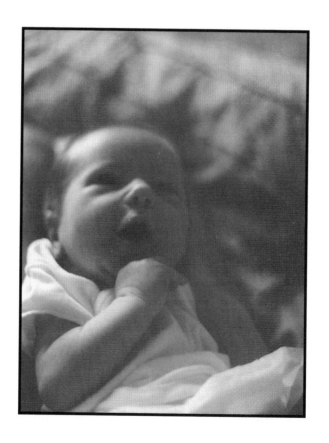

Extensions and Variations:

- In this activity, the child is learning to associate the caregiver's voice with comfort.
- The caregiver can learn which activities are comforting to the child by listening for when these sounds appear.
- As the child gets older, he will begin imitating the more complex sounds you make, and later he will imitate words.

HOME CONNECTION

Encourage families to vocalize, smile, and talk to the child to elicit these first sounds throughout the families' routines. Communicate the special activities that appear to be most comforting or enjoyable to the child in the classroom. Ask them for the home activities during which the child seems to express pleasure and sounds.

Holding Up My Head

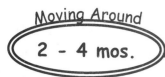

Purpose: The child holds up his head without support. Until the child learns strong, steady head control, it is important that the caregiver provide support to the child's head. When the child begins to have his own head support and control, he will begin to explore his surroundings with more interest and alertness.

Materials: none

Preparation: Hold the child in an upright position looking over your shoulder.

Activity: Carry the child from one room to the next in this position, show the child interesting things seen from this position, or have the child look into a mirror while being held in this way.

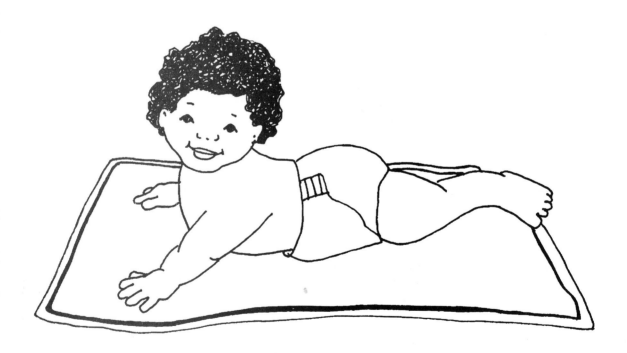

Extensions and Variations:

• Place the child in a variety of positions for short periods of time so he can practice holding up his head.

• These positions may include the child lying on his stomach, lying in a soft chair, being held in front of the caregiver facing out, swinging gently in a child swing, being carried on the caregiver's back, or riding in a child stroller.

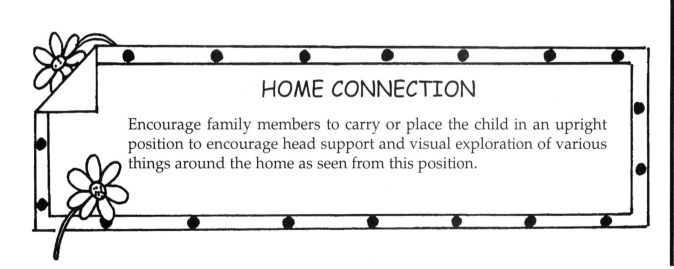

HOME CONNECTION

Encourage family members to carry or place the child in an upright position to encourage head support and visual exploration of various things around the home as seen from this position.

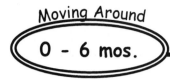
Moving Together

Purpose: The child rocks and moves with caregiver. The child learns the sensation of her body moving in different ways and at various rhythms. This activity is an important first stage before the child learns to move around by herself. She begins to develop muscle strength, movement control, balance, a sense of her body moving in space, and development of both the left and the right sides of the body.

Materials: none necessary, but a rocking chair is useful if it is available

Preparation: Hold the child on your lap, in your arms, or lie on the floor with the child in your arms.

Activity: Rock the child back and forth in a rocking chair, in your arms, or on your lap. This activity is comforting and soothing, and may be done at intervals throughout the day. You may also hold the child while you lie on your back, then rock up to a sitting position, then back down. This can be repeated several times.

Extensions and Variations:

- Play music or sing while you gently dance around the room holding the child.
- Try this with fast and slow tunes, moving to the rhythm of the music.

HOME CONNECTION

Show families how to rock the child, dance with the child, move rhythmically with the child, and let the child experience various positions while being held.

3 - 5 mos.

I Can Lift My Head!

Purpose: This activity helps the child to lift his head, so that he will be more visually alert and attentive to the things and the people around him.

Materials: none

Preparation: Place the child on his stomach on a clean blanket or towel.

Activity: Place a picture of a face or a photograph of a family member in front of the child to encourage the child to lift his head at an angle to see the picture. If the child has a rattle, favorite toy, or colorful play item, move it in front of his face to encourage head lifting.

Extensions and Variations:

- Attach some brightly colored ribbons or yarn to the child's crib board so that the child will lift his head to see them.
- Place a favorite picture or photograph of a family member inside crib on the board so that the child sees it by lifting his head.
- Place a round bolster or rolled pillow under the child's chest and arms to encourage head lifting.
- Holding the child on your lap on his stomach, roll the child back and forth, and side to side to encourage head lifting.
- Continue to play with favorite colorful and noisy toys in front of the child's face.

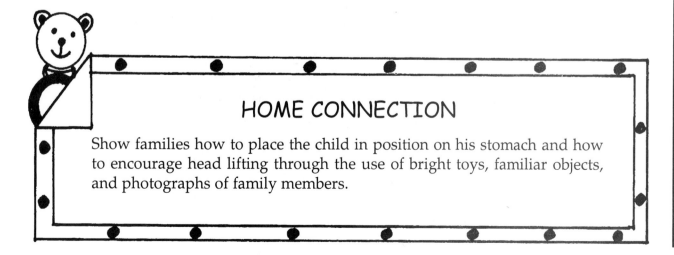

HOME CONNECTION

Show families how to place the child in position on his stomach and how to encourage head lifting through the use of bright toys, familiar objects, and photographs of family members.

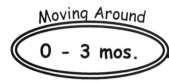

Looking Around

Purpose: The child turns her head independently. By turning her head from side to side, a baby begins to learn to rotate her head. This will later lead the child to visual exploration, to bearing weight on her arms, to shifting weight between arms, and eventually to crawling.

Materials: none

Preparation: Child may be sitting, lying in her crib, or lying on the floor on her stomach or back.

Activity: Place the child on different sides of her body when you put her down rather than always placing the child on her left or right side. Place pictures, mobiles, and toys in various places in the crib, moving them from time to time to encourage the child to turn her head to locate them. When the child is lying down not facing you, say the child's name to call her attention to you, and encourage her to turn to face you.

Extensions and Variations:

• When the child is in a soft chair, shake a rattle or ring a small bell at her side encourage the child to turn her head.
• You may also do this with a brightly colored object or light.

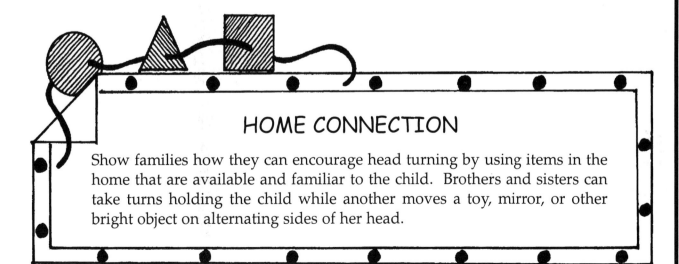

HOME CONNECTION

Show families how they can encourage head turning by using items in the home that are available and familiar to the child. Brothers and sisters can take turns holding the child while another moves a toy, mirror, or other bright object on alternating sides of her head.

Chapter Three

Eight to Eighteen Months: The Mobile Infant

What Is the Eight- to Eighteen-Month-Old Child Like?

Between eight and eighteen months of age, the mobile infant:

- Is developing a sense of who he is
- Knows that he is different from other people
- Is constantly learning how to move from crawling to walking
- Can understand language but does not talk much
- Wants to dress and feed himself although he is clumsy
- Shows happy, sad, and angry feelings. (This child shows anger at objects and people!)

When planning the classroom for mobile infants, caregivers need to remember to think about safety. Mobile infants move about quickly and touch everything. Be sure there are safe places to crawl and climb on in the classroom. Caregivers can guide mobile infants by encouraging them to play safely. When a child chews on a washcloth, say, "The washcloth is for cleaning your hands and face." Caregivers can help children develop language by labeling objects and describing their play.

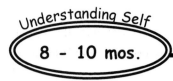

Finding Something New

Purpose: This activity offers the infant a chance to independently find toys that are of interest to him. The infant at this age can crawl and is able to move by himself. The infant works on "self-regulation" when choosing to find a toy.

Materials: two favorite infant toys for each child

Preparation:
1. Observe the infant's behavior to see if he is ready to play (alert, calm, and looking at you).
2. Choose 2 toys the infant knows and likes to play with.
3. Clear an area on the floor in the play space.
4. You may play with 2 infants at one time. Sit so you can see the play of other children in the classroom.

Activity: When the infant has just arrived in the play area or is ready for a new toy, begin the activity. Place the child's favorite toy just out of reach. Ask, "Where is the ball? Look for the ball."

Encourage the infant's attempt to move to and find the toy. You could say, "Peter, you found the ball," and "You found something to play with by crawling." Encourage the child to find new toys by himself by saying, "You wanted something new to play with. When you want a new toy, you look for another." If the child is interested in a new toy, repeat with the second toy.

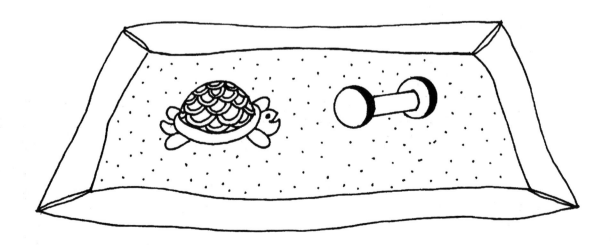

Extensions and Variations:

- To maintain interest, add a third favorite toy for the infant to find. Place this toy out of reach from where the infant is playing.
- This activity can work with a small group. Choose a favorite toy for each infant. It helps to have duplicates, for example, 2 balls or 2 small similar toys, since infants are too young for sharing.
- Instead of commercial toys, use common items from home such as wooden spoons, small pots and covers, and small containers with lids.
- Use toys with high-contrast colors such as black and white for children who have difficulty seeing.

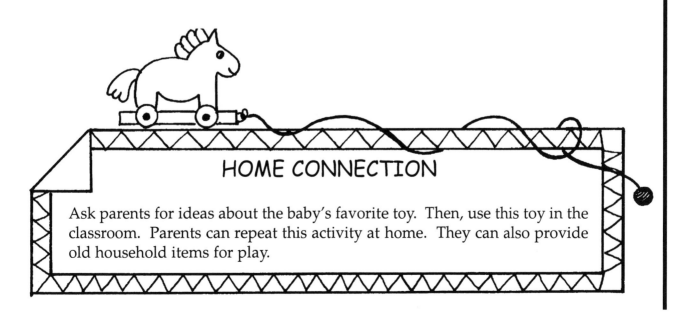

HOME CONNECTION

Ask parents for ideas about the baby's favorite toy. Then, use this toy in the classroom. Parents can repeat this activity at home. They can also provide old household items for play.

My Feelings

Purpose: The child learns to identify the emotions connected to faces that adults make. An infant at this age can recognize the 4 emotions of happy, sad, surprised, and mad. She observes the adult's face for cues on emotions.

Materials: none

Preparation:
1. Observe to see if children are ready to learn.
2. Introduce the activity by saying, "Let's play a game."
3. You can play this with 1 child or a small group of 3 children.

Activity: Begin the game by saying: "Marina, let's play a guessing game. Guess how I am feeling. Look at my face." Make a face that is happy. Encourage the child to guess how you are feeling. If the child responds, "Happy," encourage her by saying, "Marina, you are good at this game. Yes, I was making a happy face." If the child responds with an emotion other than happy, such as surprised, show her what a surprised face looks like. Repeat the happy face and ask the child again, "Guess how I am feeling. Look at my face."

Try another emotion, and continue until all 4 emotions (happy, sad, surprised and mad) are presented, or until the child loses interest.

Extensions and Variations:

- Make faces on cards or cut out pictures from an old magazine of the 4 emotions. Point to the cards one at a time and ask the child, "Guess what this person is feeling. Look at the face." After you have asked the child, she may want to point to the faces and have you respond.
- Act out the emotion with your body and face. The child can imitate your actions and provide variations. The child over 18 months will find it easier to act out the emotions.

HOME CONNECTION

Share this game with the child's parents. Observe if the parents use different behaviors to express the emotions. The parents can repeat the game at home, using their own variations of the behaviors.

Dancing With Scarves

Purpose: This activity allows the child to express emotions through dancing. As the child dances the adult can point out that feelings are connected to behaviors. The child practices control of physical movements and begins to understand the relationship of his body in space. The child observes how scarves move, and learns about cause and effect relationships. The activity also promotes language with words such as *high, low, front, back, fast,* and *slow.*

Materials: scarf for each child and adult
box or basket to put the scarves in
cassette tape or compact disk player
music of different types—both fast paced and slow
homemade tape of your children's favorite songs
classical music, marches, instrumental music
lullabies, music from different cultures
your own voice or a parent who likes to sing

Preparation: This activity works well with a group of 2 to 4 children. Children will come over and join in when they hear the music. Some will stay longer than others. If a large group comes over to play, make sure you have enough scarves.

Activity: Put on the music or begin singing. Listen to it and begin dancing and waving your scarf. Use simple motions, such as back and forth and up and down. As the music plays, hand each child a scarf. Dance with them and encourage them to wave their scarves up high and down low, fast and slow, in front and behind them.

Play a second type of music. Listen to it. Start to move your body to the new beat. Encourage the children to wave their scarves to the new music. Talk about how the music makes you feel. Quick, light sounds make you feel happy; slow, heavy sounds make you feel sad or mad; lullabies make you feel sleepy. Point out what the children are doing. "Peter is moving his scarf slowly." When the children seem to lose interest, play or sing slow music to help them calm down. When calm, ask them to return the scarves to the box or basket.

Extensions and Variations:

- Use other materials for dancing such as washcloths, bells, or streamers.
- Toddlers and two-year-olds also like this activity. They are able to listen and dance to 3 types of music. The older children enjoy this as a group activity.

HOME CONNECTION

Ask parents for ideas on music. They may offer suggestions of the family's favorite songs. Encourage parents to do this activity at home. A radio is also a good source of music, and the parent can switch the stations to find different types of music.

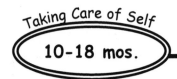

This Is the Way We Wash Our Hands

Purpose: Children sing a song as they pretend to wash their hands and brush their teeth and hair. This activity encourages self-help skills and leads to independent behavior. It also develops language skills.

Materials: picture of hands being washed
pictures of a hairbrush and toothbrush

Preparation:
1. Lay the pictures on the rug and invite the children who are nearby to come and sing.
2. This activity is best with a small group of 2 to 4 children.

Activity: Introduce the song by saying, "I have a song to sing to you today." While singing the song, hold up the picture that goes with the verse. You can make up your own music or use the music to a song such as, "Here We Go Round the Mulberry Bush."

Hold up the picture of washing hands and sing,
This is the way we wash our hands, wash our hands, wash our hands.
This is the way we wash our hands, so early in the morning.

Encourage the child to play by saying, "Alexander, show me how you wash your hands." Make up verses for brushing hair and brushing teeth.

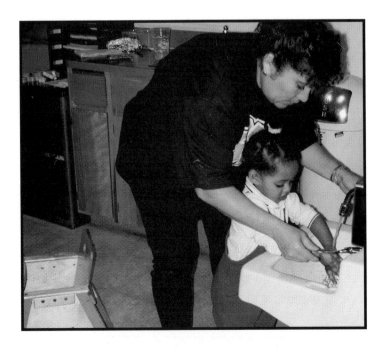

Extensions and Variations:

- Sing more verses if the children are interested. Older children will sing about dressing and eating also.
- Use another activity such as cleaning the house and include verses on ways to sweep the floor, vacuum the rug, wash the floor, wash the clothes, and wipe the table.
- Ask older children to tell you what happens first in the morning. Find or draw pictures that illustrate the sequence of washing hands, for example. Then, place the pictures in sequence and sing.
- Use this song while children wash, dress, and eat during the day.

HOME CONNECTION

Talk with the parents about the sequence they use with the child in the morning. Then, substitute the child s name in the song as you sing. "This is the way Paolo eats his breakfast." Encourage the parents to try this song as they get the child ready for coming to kindergarten.

Dressing Book

Purpose: The adult makes a book about dressing and reads it with the child. This activity is important for identifying self-help skills in dressing. It is also helpful for encouraging early speech as the child practices connecting a word with an object.

Materials: pictures of clothes: shirt, pants, jacket, sweater, socks, shoes and hat
yarn
thick paper
glue

Preparation:
1. Draw or cut out from old magazines some pictures of different items of clothing.
2. Cut the paper to make the pages—a page per piece of clothing. Glue a picture on each page. The pages can be covered with plastic or contact paper to make them more durable.
3. Make 4 holes on the side of each page for the yarn. Use the yarn to fasten the pages together, tying knots at both ends.
4. This activity works well in the book area with 2 to 3 children.

Activity: Read the book while the child is sitting on your lap or sitting near you. Point to the different pieces of clothing. Then point to the child's clothing. Ask the child to point to the article of clothing in the book and then point to the same article of clothing the child is wearing. Comment on the different colors and prints on the clothing. Some children will also be able to name the clothing in addition to pointing.

Extensions and Variations:

• Ask the older child to show or tell you where the clothing is worn by saying, "Where do the socks go?" After the child points, say, "Socks go on your feet."
• When working with 2 or 3 children, have each child point out the article of clothing.
• You could add, "Julia, you have a shirt and Josef, you also have a shirt." Ask the children, "Where do Katrina's socks go?"
• Encourage the children to dress themselves during the daily routine. Encourage them to go and get their clothes, to help by holding up their arms and pulling up their pants.

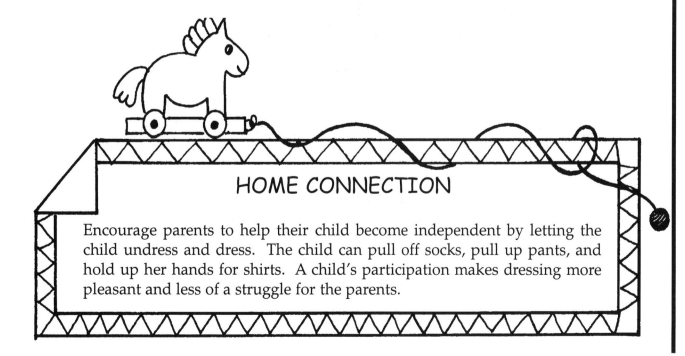

HOME CONNECTION

Encourage parents to help their child become independent by letting the child undress and dress. The child can pull off socks, pull up pants, and hold up her hands for shirts. A child's participation makes dressing more pleasant and less of a struggle for the parents.

Pouring Water

Purpose: The child practices pouring water with pitchers and cups. This activity develops the child's skills for feeding and also helps the child feel proud of his accomplishments.

Materials: small plastic pitcher for each child
2 plastic cups for each child
sensory table (small table for sand and water play) or plastic tub
smock for each child

Preparation
1. Fill the pitcher halfway with water.
2. Place the pitcher with 2 cups beside it in the sensory table or plastic tubs.
3. Place a smock where the child can see it.
4. If more children are choosing this activity, include more materials for each child.
5. This activity is good for 2 to 3 children during choice time. The adult is nearby to help. Make sure another adult is available to work with the other children in the room.

Activity: Introduce the activity to the child. "Thomas, you can pour water. Pour the water into the cups." The child will need to use both hands to hold the pitcher. This will help with control. Help the child as needed. You might hold the cup steady while the child pours. Describe what the child is doing: "Thomas, you are pouring water into the cup." If the child wants to drink the water, have some drinking water available at another table and show him this water.

Extensions and Variations:

- When the child is ready (usually toddlers and two-year-olds), put small child-sized pitchers at the table for eating and encourage the child to pour water or juice. Be ready for some spills and try not to shame the child when accidents occur. One way to avoid spilling is to have the child pour only small amounts.
- The younger child could explore cups and a spoon with no water. Demonstrate how you use a spoon or a cup and give the items back to the child.
- Add small cups and saucers to the sensory table. The child can pour pretend tea.

HOME CONNECTION

Parents are often worried about spills and are hesitant to let the young child practice with real food. You could suggest practice with water, and tell the parent that children need a lot of practice with water before they can pour the juice. You might want to find out if playing with water is considered wasteful. In this case, pouring something else might be better, such as large wooden beads or another safe material that can be poured.

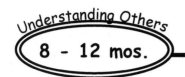
Book About Me

Purpose: The adult makes an individual book for the child. The child learns to recognize herself as a separate person.

Materials: photographs of the child and family
drawing or photograph of favorite toy
construction paper
markers
yarn
glue

Preparation:
1. Ask the family for pictures of the child and family members.
2. Draw a picture of the child's favorite toy.
3. Cut construction paper to make the pages—a page for each photograph. Glue a photograph or place a drawing on each piece of paper. The photographs or pages can be covered with plastic or contact paper to make them more durable.
4. Make 4 holes on the side of each page for the yarn. Use the yarn to fasten the pages together, tying knots at both ends.
5. Write a title on the first page, such as "A Book about Anna."

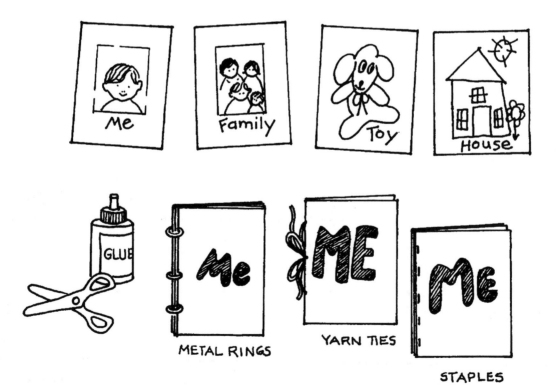

Activity: Place the child on your lap and read the book. Talk about each picture and ask, "What's this?" Describe the pictures, pointing out who or what is on each page. Describe what the child is doing. If the child is interested, read the story again.

Extensions and Variations:

• Take some pictures of the child in the classroom, and make a book about the child's day in the classroom. These pictures might include playing with a favorite toy, eating, sleeping, washing, or playing with an adult or child. These pictures will be interesting to the family and you can encourage the family to borrow the book. Read the book before nap time.
• Make a book about the infant's family.
• Make a book about "My Friends" by taking or collecting pictures of all the children in the group. Read this book to individuals or small groups. Encourage them to point to themselves and to the other children. With the older child, ask, "Who's this friend?"

HOME CONNECTION

Families may be able to contribute pictures for the books. They can borrow the book and read it at home.

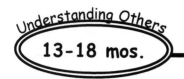

Friendship Mural

Purpose: This activity is an opportunity to draw a group picture. Children draw side-by-side, and practice parallel play. They learn social skills as they work together. The children are also practicing using small motor skills and expanding their creativity.

Materials: large piece of paper
box of toddler-size crayons
transparent tape to hold paper on the table

Preparation: 1. Clear a space on a table or the floor.
2. Cut a large piece of paper and use 2 pieces of tape to attach it to the surface.
3. Put a few crayons on the table within reach of the children.
4. This activity can be done with a small group of 2 to 4 children.

Activity: Invite the child to come draw a picture. "This paper and these crayons are for drawing. Everyone is working on this picture." If necessary, help the toddler hold the crayon. Observe the child drawing. Encourage him to draw on the paper. Describe the toddler's work: "Peter, you are making a blue line. You are making a short line."

Try to emphasize the focus of the child's drawing and not the product. Describe the colors, shape, and size of the child's marks.

As other children join in, describe them working on the same picture. As each child finishes, print his name next to his drawing. If a child tries to take another child's crayon, remind him that the other child is using the crayon. Offer another crayon to draw with. At the end of the activity, find a place to hang the picture. Ask the children to help hang the picture. Tell them, "We all worked hard. We made this picture together."

Extensions and Variations:

- Paint a friendship mural. Use small non-spill containers of paint with 2 or 3 colors. Make sure you have enough smocks. Limit the painting to 1 to 3 children.
- Use printing to make the mural. Cut some old sponges in different shapes. Place 2 colors of paint on shallow trays. The children will need smocks. Demonstrate how to place the sponge in the paint and then on the paper.

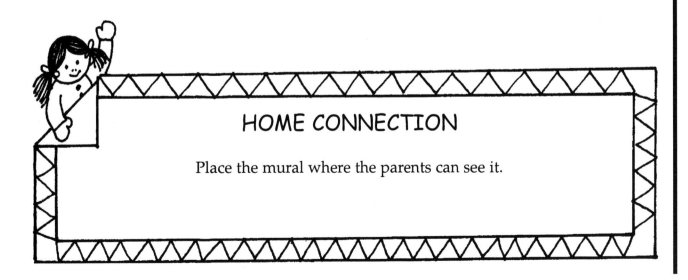

HOME CONNECTION

Place the mural where the parents can see it.

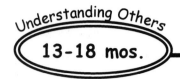
Our Coloring Box

Purpose: The children color a large box as a group. This activity encourages parallel play. The children learn how to be members of a group through coloring together. This activity also allows children to use markers and to develop creativity.

Materials: large cardboard box
box of felt tip markers
2 containers to hold markers

Preparation: 1. Clear an area that can be carefully supervised.
2. Place the box in the cleared area and place the containers of markers on either end of the box. Place the same colors in each container.
3. A small group of 2 to 3 children is best for this activity.

Activity: Invite the children to color the large cardboard box. Help them remove the tops of the markers. They might also need assistance putting the caps on the markers. Observe the children's work with the markers. Remind them that the markers should stay near the box so that they do not carry the markers around the classroom. Describe the work being done by each child. Mobile infants' first marks, or designs are important examples of creativity and physical development. You might describe the child's choice of color, the size and shape of the marks and her use of the space. Describe how the children are working together. "Marina and Julia are working at the same time." As each child finishes coloring, print her name next to her drawing on the box. Finish the activity for each child by saying, "Everyone worked together to color the box."

Display the finished box in the classroom so everyone can admire it.

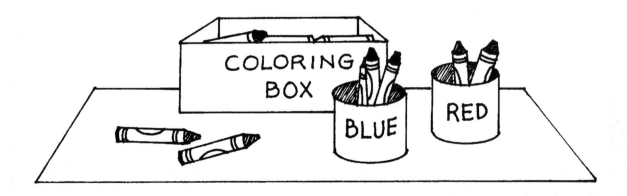

Extensions and Variations:

- Cover the box with paper and tape the paper in place. This provides a cleaner surface.
- Have children work on smaller, paper-covered boxes individually and then display all the boxes on a shelf.
- Use paint instead of markers.
- Children can crawl inside and decorate the interior of the box.
- Take this activity outside and offer it as a group activity.

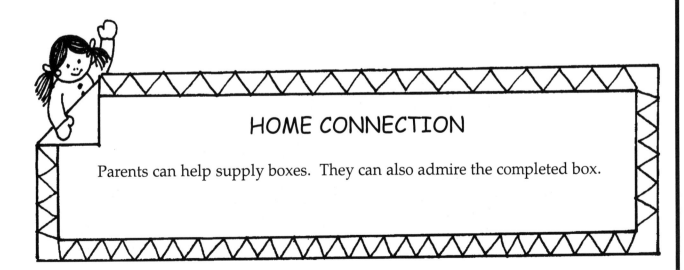

HOME CONNECTION

Parents can help supply boxes. They can also admire the completed box.

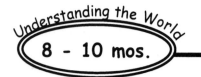

I Can Find It

Purpose: The adult hides a toy in a box and the child finds it. This activity encourages object permanence in which the child learns that the object exists even if she cannot see it. The mobile infant also practices observing objects.

Materials: box
materials for packaging—small pieces of cloth or paper (Use material that is too large to swallow.)
small toys or objects—for example, small cars, rattles, or balls

Preparation: 1. Place packaging material in the box and hide an object in the box.
2. Find a place to sit on the floor and play.
3. This activity can be done with a small group of 1 to 3 infants during play time.

Activity: Tell the child you have a game to play. Demonstrate how to find the toy. Have the child find the object. Then add more objects and encourage the child to find more things. If you have more than one child, put several small objects in the box and let 2 or 3 children look at the same time. Describe the play as the children look for objects.

Extensions and Variations:

- Larger objects make this game easier and help children who have difficulty grasping. When you hide the object, let the child see part of it. This is good for children who have difficulty seeing.
- Use smaller objects to make this activity more difficult for older children. Use more packaging material so objects are harder to find.
- Hide an object in your hand and switch it from hand to hand. Let the child guess which hand the object is in. Then, let the child hide the object.
- Hide objects in a shoe box without packaging materials. Put the lid on a shoe box to hide the object.

HOME CONNECTION

Parents can play this game with a box at home. Loan the box to them if they do not have one. Encourage older siblings to play this game with the child.

Building a Tower

Purpose: The adult makes simple blocks and the child builds a tower with them. Playing with blocks is fun and is important for later problem solving and skills in mathematics. Young children learn about balance, height, weight, and size as they play. At this age, light blocks are easier for building.

Materials: clean cardboard juice or milk containers—small, medium, and large, at least 2 of each size.
scissors or a sharp knife
plastic or contact paper to cover the blocks (optional)

Preparation: 1. Cut off the top portion of the container on the fold.
2. Take 2 containers and push together the open ends to make the block.
3. Cut some larger containers in half. This makes some blocks that are cubes.
4. The blocks can be covered with plastic or contact paper or left as they are.
5. Build a tower with 1 or 2 children.

Activity: Use these blocks during play time. Sit on the floor with the child and begin stacking the blocks. Children this age can successfully stack 3 blocks with practice, so try to limit your tower to 3 blocks. Encourage the child to build with you. Start with a few large blocks with the younger child. The child may just want to knock down the blocks you build at first. Encourage the child to put one block on top of another. You might encourage the child by saying, "Josef, you are building with blocks. You are putting a block on top of another block. What a good builder."

Extensions and Variations:

- As the children get better at building, add 2 more blocks.
- Try to have 2 sets of blocks so more than 1 child can build.
- Add small cars and figures to the child's play with blocks. The blocks can become buildings for the cars to drive around. The figures can live in the buildings.

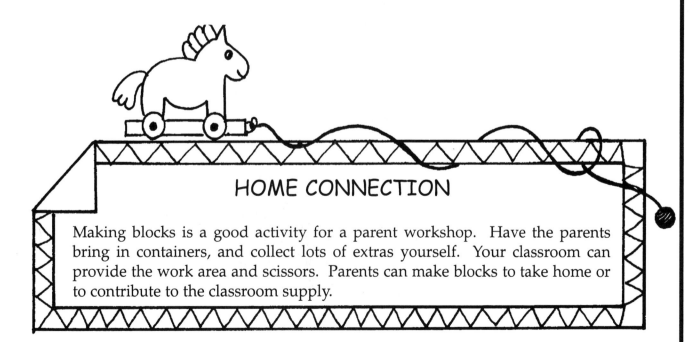

HOME CONNECTION

Making blocks is a good activity for a parent workshop. Have the parents bring in containers, and collect lots of extras yourself. Your classroom can provide the work area and scissors. Parents can make blocks to take home or to contribute to the classroom supply.

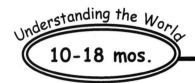

Circle Shape Drop

Purpose: The child drops circles into a slot in a lid. This activity develops the understanding of object permanence and the child learns about the circle shape. The activity also promotes small motor control. The child learns how to solve problems.

Materials: cardboard container with a lid (e.g., oatmeal box)
2-3 juice can lids or thick paper cut in circles

Preparation:
1. Cut a slot in the lid of the cardboard container so that the circles can fit easily through the slot.
2. Make sure the lids are smooth on the edges and safe for play.
3. Cover the container with paper to make it attractive.
4. Use this activity at play time with 1 or 2 children.

Activity: Invite the child to play the circle game. Show the child how to put the circle in the container. As he tries, encourage his work by saying, "You are putting the circle in the slot very carefully. You put the circle in the slot. Good job!" To develop the understanding of object permanence, after the circles are in the box, ask the child, "Mark, where are the lids?"

Extension and Variations:

• Use objects of different shapes cut from plastic lids or try using cookie cutters in simple shapes. Start with 3 shapes: the circle, square, and triangle. Cut holes in the plastic large enough for the shapes. Encourage the child to use the shape.   "Josef, you are holding a square. It has 4 sides. Find the square place on the box. Put the square through the square hole."   You might need to suggest that the child match the hole and the shape before dropping the shape in the hole.

• The child may want to work independently without your help. This is an activity where a child can work alone. Make 2 shape sorters for 2 children to work with at the same time.

• Add more shapes as the child is ready.

HOME CONNECTION

Make a list of circular items that can be found in the home. Encourage the parents to point these circles out to the child. Some examples are the faces of clocks and watches, lids of pots, and bottoms of cans and bottles.

Sorting Shapes

Purpose: The child sorts shapes into different containers. This activity encourages children to identify objects that are different and those that are similar. The child learns to categorize similar objects. This type of sorting is important for later learning and is also helpful for learning shapes.

Materials: 2 or 3 objects of simple shapes—squares, triangles, and circles—use puzzle pieces, small wooden blocks, or make shapes from thick paper or plastic lids
3 small bowls for shape sorting
clear bowl for all of the shapes

Preparation: 1. Make or assemble the shapes.
2. Place the small bowls for shape sorting on either side of the clear bowl.
3. Clear a space in the play area. This activity works well near other manipulative toys. One or two children may work at this activity. Other children may be playing next to this activity with other similar toys you have set out, for example, a few action toys, building blocks, or puzzles.

Activity: Invite any child who appears interested to play. "Nina, look at these shapes." You could describe the objects and point out the circles and squares and triangles. Observe the child exploring the shapes. You could suggest that she sort the shapes into the bowls. Try to follow the child's lead in sorting. If the child is holding a circle, take another circle and place it in a bowl. Ask the child to place her circle in the bowl. You might describe the play by saying, "We put the circles in the bowl." Then watch the child pick up another shape and say, "Nina, let's place the triangle in this bowl." Put the shape in a separate bowl. As you work, encourage the child. Some comments might include: "Nina, you are sorting the shapes in the bowls. You did it."

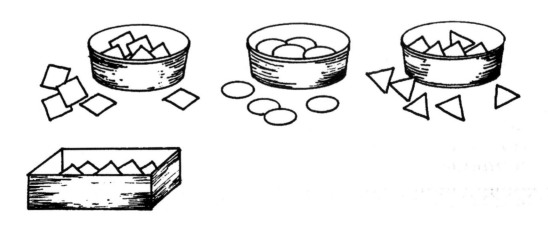

Encourage but do not push the child. Some children will just explore the shapes and not be interested in sorting. If you offer this experience a second or third time their interest in sorting will grow after the material is more familiar.

Extensions and Variations:

- Use other objects for sorting, for example, small trucks in one bowl and small cars in the other.
- To sort by color, have objects of different colors, for example 5 blue cars and 5 red cars, or 5 red circles and 5 blue circles. To make the activity easier, sort the red objects into a red bowl and the blue objects into a blue bowl.

HOME CONNECTION

Tell the parents about the importance of sorting objects. This is an activity that children will begin practicing as infants and continue through the years of preschool.

Nesting Cans

Purpose: The child places small cans inside of larger cans. This activity helps the child see differences in sizes, and practice with small motor skills. The activity also encourages classifying by size: small, medium, and large.

Materials: small, medium, and large cans
cloth tape or other strong tape to cover the edges of the can
pliers to pinch down sharp points on the cans

Preparation: 1. Check the cans for sharp edges. Pinch down any sharp spots with pliers.
2. Cover the edges of the cans with cloth tape.
3. Find an open space in the play area and sit down.
4. Do this activity with 1 to 2 children during play time.

Activity: Invite a child who appears interested in the cans to come play by saying, "Let's put the small can in the big can." The adult starts the activity by giving the child the smallest can. The adult places the first 2 cans and the child can put the smallest one inside. Next, suggest the child put the small one in the medium can. Then suggest the child place both in the large can. You might place the first can to help the child get started. Some children will be able to place only 1 can to start.

Two children can nest the cans with your help. Each child can place one can in another. They will need your help deciding who goes first.

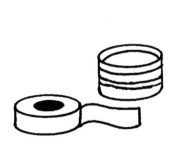

Extensions and Variations:

- Try building a tower with the cans. At first the child will only be able to put the smallest can on top of the 2 larger cans. With help from you and practice, the child will be able to use all 3 cans.
- Make this more challenging by adding 2 more cans between the largest and smallest sizes.
- Find an object that just fits inside the medium-sized can. Let the child put it in the can and take it out. Ask the child to put it in the small can. When it doesn't fit say, "Too big." Repeat this game by putting the object in the big can and say, "Too little." Then try the medium-sized can again saying, "Just right." This game allows the child to explore size relationships and gives him the words to describe different sizes.
- Use measuring cups and spoons for nesting.

HOME CONNECTION

Families can help by saving a set of cans or boxes of different sizes. After you make the nesting cans, encourage parents to do the activity at home with the young child. You might send home a set and keep two in the classroom. The child can have lots of practice with the activity.

Bear's Visit

Purpose: The child learns words in a game with a stuffed animal or puppet. This activity promotes language skills and vocabulary. The children can learn names of body parts as well as words such as fur, bear, tail, tickle, touch, and hug.

Materials: stuffed bear or bear puppet

Preparation:
1. Find a space to sit and share the bear activity with 1 or 2 children. Others may join the activity as they hear you.
2. Observe to see who is interested and invite a child to play.

Activity: Show the child or children the stuffed bear or puppet. Talk about the animal's tail or furry body. Say the following verse:

> *A bear came to visit me!*
> *He thought I was a tree.*
> *First he sat on my knee.* (Point to your knee)
> *Then he climbed down to my toes.* (Crawl the bear from your leg to your toes)
> *Oh no, now he's looking at my nose!* (Point to nose)

Try this song using the child's body. Have the bear pretend to tickle or hug different parts of the child's body. Say, "The bear is going to tickle your leg now," as the bear touches the child's leg. Have the bear touch other parts of the body like the fingers and arms.

Extensions and Variations:

- Use other stuffed animals.
- Older children may like to sit in a small group and say the verse with you. Use the children's names, " A bear came to visit Anna." Do this with each child who is willing. You could also show them a picture of the animal before you begin and point out the parts of the animal including the tail, fur, feathers, or beak.

HOME CONNECTION

Teach this activity to the parents either at a parent meeting or when they come to get their child. Encourage them to try this game at home, using a different stuffed animal.

Making Animal Sounds

Purpose: The adult makes or reads a book about animals and encourages the child to make animal sounds. This activity helps the child learn new words and sounds. The child learns how to respond to questions, through interacting with the caregiver.

Materials: book with familiar animals such as farm animals or household pets
pictures of animals—cut from magazines or drawn
heavy paper for pages
glue
plastic or contact paper
yarn or strong string

Preparation: 1. Cut out or draw pictures of animals.
2. Cut out pages from construction paper, enough for an animal on each page.
3. Glue a picture on each page.
4. Cover the pages with plastic or contact paper to make them durable.
5. Attach the pages by cutting 4 or 5 holes on the left-hand side and lacing them with string.

This activity works well with an individual and small groups of 4.

Activity: When the book is made, choose a space near other books. Wait for a child to choose the book. Offer to read the book to the child. If the child agrees by nodding his head or handing you the book, sit down with the child and begin reading. While reading, ask questions about the picture. "Peter, what is this animal?" If the child does not have the word for the animal, say it for him. Ask, "What sound does a duck make?" Encourage the child by saying, "Yes, a duck says quack." Read the book again if he is interested. Read the book to others who have joined you. Leave the book in the play area for other children to look at.

Extensions and Variations:

• Sing a song with animal sounds. (A popular American song is called "Old MacDonald." The lyrics are in the activity "Animal Stick Puppets," Chapter 6.)
• Choose other books with animals in them and ask the child to identify the animal and the sound it makes.
• Make simple animals out of felt. Place these on the felt board and ask the child to tell you the type of animal and its sounds. (See the following activity for instructions on how to make a felt board.)

HOME CONNECTION

Find out what animals the child has seen. Try to include these in your book. Tell the parents which animals you are learning about in the classroom.

Bumblebee Sounds

Purpose: The child sings about bumblebees and learns about them. This activity encourages the child to learn the words for the bees' house and practice bee sounds. The child also learns the names for body parts.

Materials: large picture of bumblebee or bumblebee made out of felt
pieces of felt—large and small
glue
large piece of cardboard

Preparation:
1. Make a bumblebee out of felt by drawing on felt.
2. Make a simple hive out of felt.
3. Make a felt board by gluing a large piece of felt on the piece of cardboard.
4. Children might do this individually or in a small group of up to 4.

Activity: Find a place to sit with the felt board, perhaps near other books and language materials. Sing the simple song for children (make up your own music):

Bumble, bumble, bumblebee buzz
Flew out of the hive
And landed right under Marina's chin
Buzzzzzzz, Buzzzzzz, Buzzzz! (Softly tickle child's chin)

Repeat the song using different children's names. Use the bumblebee felt board with the song. First, place the hive and then the bumblebee on the board. Children might want to put the bumblebee on the felt board as you sing.

Extensions and Variations:

- Use other flying creatures such as butterflies with flowers or birds.
- Change the words of the song to include other body parts.
- With older children use different types of birds to develop the child's vocabulary.

HOME CONNECTION

Teach the song to the parents. You could write it down and place it on the bulletin board or sing it when they arrive. Find out what types of insects and birds the family sees and include these in the song.

Texture Book

Purpose: The adult presents a book with different textures. This activity promotes speech and helps the child to connect a word with a sense experience.

Materials: squares of different fabric, such as flannel, corduroy, fake fur, and smooth polyester
cardboard or index cards for each piece of fabric plus 2 additional cards
glue
hole punch
marker
key ring

Preparation:
1. Glue each piece of fabric to an index card.
2. Punch a hole in the upper left-hand corner of each index card.
3. Write a title for the texture book on an index card. The last card can be illustrated or left blank.
4. Place the index cards in order beginning with the title card and ending with the blank card. Hold the cards together by inserting the key ring through the hole in each card.
5. This book can be read to a child during choice time.

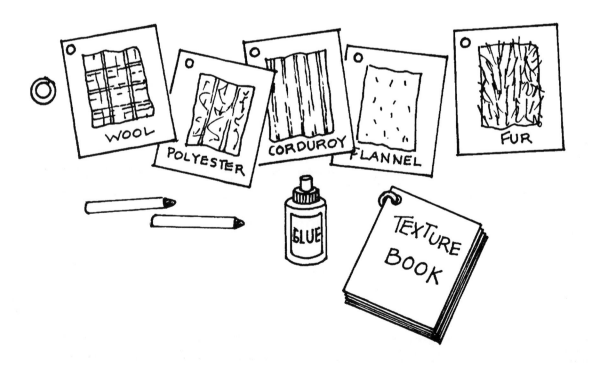

Activity: Place the book on the shelf with other books or find an open space on the floor and place the book on the floor. When a child selects the book, observe what the child touches. Describe the sense experience of the different textures. "Alexander, this is very smooth." "This is very bumpy."

Ask the child "How does this feel on your fingers?" You could also ask, "What else does this feel like?" Respond to the child's language, by saying, for example, "Yes, that is soft."

Extensions and Variations:

- Use other objects such as sand and sandpaper for rough textures, and glue or smooth paper for smooth ones. To be safe, cover the sand with contact paper.
- Adults can make a texture walk inside. Use thick and thin pieces of carpet, the smooth floor, and a piece of sandpaper (or a piece of paper with sand glued to it).
- Tape the pieces to the floor. Lead 2 children down the walk and talk about how it feels in socks or bare feet.
- The younger child (8 to 12 months) will enjoy looking at the book. Describe the texture on each page, and the child will learn the words for the sensation.
- You can also do a texture or touch walk with a child who is not yet walking. Walk around the room holding the child and have him touch different surfaces.

HOME CONNECTION

Parents can help save pieces of fabric or carpet squares. They can try a texture walk in the park near their home. The touch walk can be done inside their home.

Finding Objects

Purpose: The adult points to objects in the room and the child labels them. This activity helps develop speech. The child learns to connect words to objects.

Materials: none

Preparation: 1. You can play this game in different areas of the room. You might play on the floor with 1 to 4 children.
2. This game can be played as you walk from one room to another or outside.

Activity: Begin by saying, "There are many things around us and we are going to point to them and find them." Point to something everyone can see such as the rug or a light and name the object. Then point to something and ask, "Julia, what is that?" When the child responds, "Rug," you can repeat, "That is a rug." If the child points without speaking, you might add the word and say, "You pointed your finger at the rug."

Take turns pointing, first you and then the child. Modify this for different children. For the child who knows a lot of words, ask the child to label familiar objects. Encourage the use of new words by pointing to unfamiliar objects. Have the child with a limited vocabulary point at an object, you label it and then encourage the child to repeat the object's name. Continue for as long as the child remains interested.

Extensions and Variations:

• This activity can be done during routines of dressing and eating. It is a good way to keep the group's attention while waiting.

• For older children, try doing this activity with flashlights during free play. Have 2 flashlights and tape shut the opening of each to keep the batteries inside. Explain to the children that the flashlight can find objects. Shine the flashlight on a familiar object and say, "There is a chair in the light. Now it's your turn. What can you put in the light?" Observe the children and talk with them about what is in the light. Encourage verbal labeling of objects. For children with a limited vocabulary, identify the objects they shine the light on.

HOME CONNECTION

Suggest this activity to parents. It can be played at home or when traveling to preschool.

Puppet Games

Purpose: The adult makes a puppet and plays with the child. Puppet play is valuable because when the child plays, he practices understanding language and speaking. Puppets also encourage beginning pretend play. Puppets at this age should be simple and represent familiar figures such as animals and people. Remember that the child at this age believes the puppet is real.

Materials: familiar animal or people puppets
2-3 sock puppets easily made with:
 socks
 markers
 yarn
 needle and thread

Preparation: To make a sock puppet:
1. Take a sock and make eyes with a marker.
2. For hair, sew lengths of yarn at the end of the sock's toe or along the edge.
3. Draw a mouth at the toe end of the sock or sew a mouth with cloth.
4. Do this activity with up to 3 children.

Activity: Have at least 3 puppets available and find a place to sit. Put your hand inside a short sock and transform it magically into a creature with a mouth. With the sock on your hand, talk with a child who appears interested. Start by being the leader and have the child respond to your puppet.

Encourage the child to put a puppet on his hand and use the puppet to talk with you or another child. You will need to be a major part of the play as children have not yet developed enough speech and pretend play to do this themselves. Lead the play at first, suggesting play themes and words, and if they seem to enjoy this, continue.

With a small group of children, suggest that they play together with similar puppets, for example 2 or 3 animal puppets.

Extensions and Variations:

- Put the puppets on empty liquid soap containers. The child can manipulate the soap containers and this is easier than placing his hand inside the puppet.
- Make puppets to represent animals in a favorite book. Children will be familiar with them.
- Stuffed animals can be used in the same manner as puppets.

HOME CONNECTION

Parents can bring in old or mismatched socks to make puppets. They might have old soap dispensers as well. Older children in the family could make puppets and play with the younger child.

Push Toys

Purpose: The adult shows the child how to use push toys. This activity offers the child experience in using different senses together, for example, looking and touching. The child uses large motor skills when she goes after the rolling object. Small motor skills are needed to grasp an object.

Materials: 1 small- or medium-sized ball for each child (made of cloth so it rolls slowly)
small car or truck
container for toys

Preparation: 1. Find a protected space, away from active play, to sit.
2. Bring the toys to the space in the container.
3. Play with 1 to 3 children.

Activity: Invite the children to play with the toys. The child may first want to explore the toy by touching or mouthing it. Then roll the toy just a little out of reach. Encourage the child to crawl after the toy. As the child reaches the toy, push it a little further away. Then suggest the child push it. You might say, "Julia, you push the ball."

Some children might be frustrated and not ready to push the toy. In this case, allow them to catch the toy and fully explore it. Others will smile and look directly at you when they are ready to push. Begin by helping to push the toy. Move it slowly so the child can crawl and reach it easily. Choose toys that move slowly, for example, balls with soft textures such as cloth, and small cars with small wheels.

Extensions and Variations:

- Choose toys that move quickly such as balls with a hard surface. This activity is fun for children who can walk or crawl quickly. A small push will cause this ball to move farther and faster. Encourage the child to follow the ball as quickly as possible.
- For the child who has difficulty crawling or seeing, keep the toy very close to the child. Help the child find or reach the toy and congratulate her on reaching the toy. You might choose a favorite toy for the child to encourage her.
- Use a foam pad and foam ramp. The child crawls up the ramp to get a toy and then rolls the toy down the ramp. Encourage the child to go after the toy that has rolled. Two children can play with the ramp; one can roll the toy down the ramp and the other can crawl after the toy.

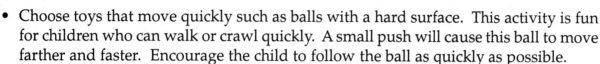

HOME CONNECTION

Ask the parents about the child's favorite toys. Use these toys to encourage the child to play this game. Ask if family members play this game and how they do it. Check with the parents to see if the child is progressing by moving farther to get the toy or pushing the toy farther.

Pull Toys

Purpose: The child learns to pull a variety of toys. This activity improves the use of eye-hand coordination while walking. Pulling toys is a challenge to a beginning walker since she must walk and hold on to the toy at the same time. The child learns about the position of the toy and her own body.

Materials: variety of pull toys—commercial or made
pull toy made by attaching a string to a small train car or truck
simple pull toys made of:
    shoe boxes or other boxes of similar size
    thick string or rope

Preparation:
1. Insert thick string or rope (less than 33 cm or 13 inches in length) through one end of the box.
2. Leave the box empty for the younger child. The older toddler (18 months and older) will fill the box with blocks, stuffed animals, and other toys.
3. Find a space to play and provide 3 or 4 simple pull toys. This space could be in an area with other types of active play. Children will move throughout the play space as they pull the toys.

Activity: Introduce the pull toys to a child who is looking at them. You could demonstrate how to pull the toys from both standing and sitting positions. Pull the toys with the child to get started. Once a child shows you she can pull a toy, suggest that she take the toy to a specific location. Begin with a location close to the child. When she can reach the location, suggest one farther away. Let her show you a place to pull the toy.

Extensions and Variations:

- Make a train by attaching two boxes that can be pulled. The child can pull and make train sounds.
- Let the children place objects in the boxes. They can use light objects such as cut-up sponges and heavy objects such as blocks. Talk about how it feels to pull the objects of different weights.
- Take pull toys outside for play. Children will discover they pull differently on different surfaces, such as sand, dirt, and cement. They can collect leaves or small stones to pull in the boxes. The outside environment is rougher and the boxes will not last long, so take them outside when they are almost worn out.

HOME CONNECTION

Parents can help supply boxes to make the pull toys. If a parent works in a store where shoes are sold, she may be able to find a lot of boxes.

Creeping and Crawling

Purpose: The child crawls and creeps in an obstacle course and along a path. This activity encourages large motor coordination and the developing skills of seeing and touching. The child learns how to solve problems as he moves around and meets obstacles.

Materials: obstacles—boxes, chairs, hoops
tape crawl—colored tape or masking tape

Preparation:
1. Prepare for one of these experiences at a time. You might begin with the obstacle crawl and do this 2 or 3 times until the children need a new crawl.
2. Choose a space where active play occurs. You can do this with a small group of up to 4 children. Make sure the fast crawlers go first.
3. Prepare the obstacle crawl by placing 3 items in a line for children to crawl/creep around or through. Try to have 3 different experiences such as crawling around the chair, through the box, and over the hoop.
4. Make a path with tape for the tape crawl. The path can be a circle or line. Start with a line path and make a circle path another time.

Activity: Invite the child to creep and crawl. You may begin the activity by demonstrating and encouraging him to follow. Describe his activity as he is doing it, by saying, "Josef, you are creeping around the chair. You are creeping toward the box. You are creeping through the box."

Some children will try only once and others will repeat the activity again and again. If more than one child is present, encourage them to crawl in the same direction.

Extensions and Variations:

- Play music to suggest a rhythm to the children.
- Older children (over 15 months) can add pretend play and do a turtle crawl. They can crawl on their hands and knees with a small blanket for a shell.
- Pretend to be other animals and reptiles—elephants, snakes, etc.
- Plan an outside texture or obstacle crawl or creep. The textures and obstacles can be natural materials.

HOME CONNECTION

Some families may have observed their child crawl and creep around furniture. Encourage them to set up a simple obstacle path with cushions and chairs. This is a good indoor winter activity.

Dumping and Filling

Purpose: The child fills and empties containers with small blocks. The "dump and fill" experiences improve the child's eye-hand coordination. The child is beginning to learn about measurement and size. As she moves objects, she is learning about concepts of "empty" and "full." The activity is also emotionally satisfying and improves the child's sense of self.

Materials: dish pans
small wooden beads or blocks, or small plastic beads*
plastic measuring cups and measuring spoons

*Use objects large enough so as not to be a swallowing hazard.

Preparation: 1. Place the dish pans on the floor in an area with other manipulative play.
2. Put blocks or beads in the pans about as deep as an adult's thumb.
3. Work with 1 to 2 children at a time.

Activity: Place the dish pans in front of a child who looks interested and encourage the child to fill and empty the pan. The child might like to explore the material first. The younger child will empty and fill one dish pan. After mastering this in one pan, the child could dump and fill from one pan to another. Two children can work face-to-face or they could each have their own dish pan.

Extensions and Variations:

- Use sand to fill and empty containers for the child over 15 months. This activity is not appropriate for younger children who will try to eat the sand.
- Use water. Place the dish pans on a vinyl tablecloth and have sponges or cloths available for large spills. There will be lots of spills since the child is practicing pouring and filling, but does not have enough coordination to do this well.

HOME CONNECTION

Parents may have observed their child playing with measuring cups and spoons in the classroom. Encourage them to set up this activity at home. They could add small objects from home to dump and fill. Remind them to use objects that are large enough so the child does not choke.

Rolling Balls

Purpose: The child and adult roll the ball to each other. The child learns the concept of rolling and practices the physical skills of rolling a ball to another person. The child also learns to take turns rolling the ball.

Materials: small- or medium-sized ball

Preparation:
1. Find a space indoors or outdoors where you can sit with a child.
2. Sit and a make a V-shape with your legs. Have the child sit with her feet touching your feet. This makes a closed-in space for the ball game.
3. Play this game with 1 child at a time.

Activity: Roll the ball to the child and say, "Here comes the ball. Can you roll it back to me?" Encourage the child to roll the ball gently. You can give her words for the different types of rolling such as slow, fast, gentle, and hard. The child can learn to roll the ball "inside the legs." Take turns rolling the ball until the child tires of the game.

Extensions and Variations:

- Use a large ball for the child who has difficulty seeing or moving her arms.
- Use smaller balls for the older child. This is a good activity for the child who is interested in balls but cannot control her throw. Rolling the ball is good practice for aiming the ball.
- Try this activity with 2 children. Older children find this game fun to play with peers. Help the children by telling them who to roll it to. At first, each child will want to roll to you. After they become familiar with the game, they will roll to each other. This interaction encourages social skills.

HOME CONNECTION

Balls are a favorite plaything. Find out what ball games the parents play with their child and play these games in the classroom. Share this activity with the parents.

Throwing Balls

Purpose: The child throws balls in a box or basket. This experience offers practice at throwing objects and coordinating movements of the eyes and hands. Throwing at a target is a difficult skill to master and this activity helps a child begin to learn this skill.

Materials: 6 small balls such as tennis balls
box or basket with large opening

Preparation:
1. Find a clear area either inside or outside. Place the box or basket next to a wall.
2. Place the balls on the ground near the box.
3. This activity works well with a small group of 2 to 4 children.

Activity: When the child crawls or walks over to the area, introduce the activity. "Daniel, this a game. Throw the balls in the box." Show the child how to throw the ball in the box. When he throws the ball, describe the activity and compliment his work. If the child drops the ball without throwing help him learn how to release his hand at the right time. This skill takes practice.

Extensions and Variations:

- Use large balls to practice using large muscles.
- Use bean bags.
- Make a sock ball. Cut off the toe part of the sock about 5 inches or 12 cm from the toe of an adult sock. Stuff the toe part of the sock with the cut-off part to the sock. Sew the open edge of the stuffed toe.
- Challenge the older children (over 2 years) by making them throw from a short distance.
- For older children, make an animal face on the bottom of a large box. Cut a hole for the mouth. Lean the box against the wall and ask the children to toss the ball in the mouth. This activity is called "feeding the animal."

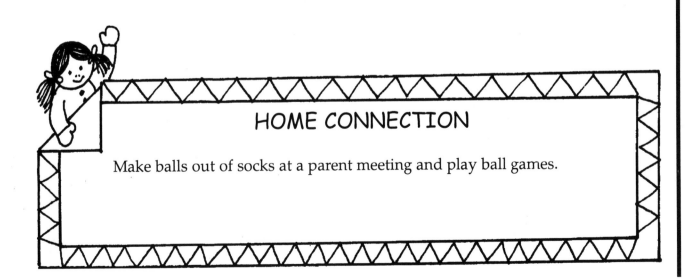

HOME CONNECTION

Make balls out of socks at a parent meeting and play ball games.

Clothespin Boxes

Purpose: The child places clothespins on the edge of a container. This activity helps improve small motor coordination. Holding the clothespin with a "pincer grasp" is practice for holding a pencil later on. The child practices eye-hand coordination.

Materials: shoe boxes
10 clothespins (It is simplest to start with peg clothespins.)

Preparation: 1. Find a clear space for the activity near other manipulative toys.
2. Place the clothespins in the box except for one that you clip on the rim as an example.
3. This activity is good for a child or 2 children at a time, so make sure there are other similar toys nearby, such as puzzles or other manipulatives.

Activity: As a child approaches, explain the activity by saying, "This clothespin goes on the edge of the box like this. Can you put the other clothespins on the edge?" Allow the child to work independently. Help the child as needed. You can support her work by praising her, "Nina, you are working hard."

You could count the clothespins the child places on the box while pointing to each one. This encourages basic number concepts, in this case, "one-to-one correspondence." When the child appears to be finished, encourage her to put the clothespins back in the box.

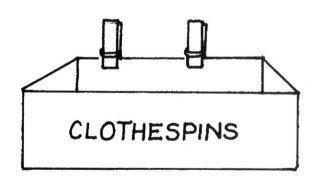

CLOTHESPINS

Extensions and Variations:

• Use a round plastic container or bucket instead of a box.
• For children who are ready, offer the squeeze-type clothespins. You will need to be available to help them at first as this activity is challenging.

HOME CONNECTION

This activity can be done at home. Find out if the family uses clothespins. If so, they may be able to use their own. Clothespins may be clipped to an empty cereal box or a large plastic container.

Chapter Four:

Eighteen to Twenty-Four Months: The Toddler

What Is the Eighteen- to Twenty-Four-Month-Old Child Like?

The child at this age is beginning to explore the world and become much more active in understanding how things work. He is learning how to communicate with adults and other children. He is also showing a new independence. The eighteen- to twenty-four-month-old child will enjoy many kinds of movement with his whole body and with his hands and fingers. He will show a lot of activity and energy. He will be curious about the world, and he will come to you with many questions. Children at this age love moving to music and learning names of things.

Here are a few major characteristics of the eighteen- to twenty-four-month-old:

- Often says "no" to some foods, to going to bed, and to simple requests
- Knows himself in the mirror, and begins to use the words "I" and "me"
- Walks, runs, and climbs into chairs
- May show some interest in using the toilet rather than a diaper
- Will play next to other children but usually not with them
- Uses many new words to talk about people, activities, and things, often putting words together for a simple sentence, such as, "Mommy go" or "Me eat."

When planning the classroom for a child this age, remember to think about leaving room for active movement as well as hand toys such as shape puzzles. Have puzzles and other interesting things in the classroom for children to explore. Make sure each child has a place of his own, such as a small storage box or coat-hanging area. Children can keep their own things in this space. Allow the children to make their own choices whenever they can, such as saying, "Would you like the red ball or the blue one?" or "Would you like to eat your soup with a big spoon or a little one?" Be sure there are musical toys in the classroom, such as rattles, drums, and bells. Go on walks in the outdoor areas around you, and talk about all the things you are seeing. Name foods, toys, clothing, and people.

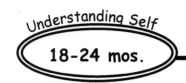

I Know My Name

Purpose: The child will say his first name either when asked, "What is your name?" or spontaneously, in referring to himself.

Materials: 2 toy telephones

Preparation: This activity can be done during any daily activity, but it can also be done using 2 toy telephones.

Activity: Using a toy telephone, pretend to call the child so that he answers on the other telephone. Ask, "Who is this?" or "Is this Alex?" Encourage the child to say his name into the telephone by playfully saying, "This sounds like Grandpa--are you sure you are Alex?"

Say the child's name often during the day. For example, tell the child, "I am putting Peter's shoes on him now!" or "I am giving Peter his dinner now!" When the child uses a word or gestures, such as pointing to an object, expand on this by saying, "Marina wants the new book" or "Eva wants to come with me to the garden." Ask questions that lead the child to say his own name, such as, "Who is wearing these mittens?" "Who is sitting on Grandmother's lap?" or "Who is eating the bowl of hot soup?" Ask the child, "Who is that?" when looking in a mirror, or when looking at a picture of the child.

Extensions and Variations:

- With the toy telephone, say things like "Hello, may I speak to Grandmother? May I speak to Daddy? Who am I speaking to?"
- If the child does not respond with his name, prompt him by saying, "I am speaking to Alex!" then repeat the game.
- Continue to state the child's name if he does not give it in these turn-taking games.
- When older or younger children join in this activity, use their names and encourage the use of each name by the group of children.
- Wait after each question to give the child time to respond with his name before saying the name for him.
- Be playful, making up a silly name and asking if it is his name: "Is your name Beezyboo? No? Timinini? No? Is it Julio? Yes! I think it is Julio! What is it?"

HOME CONNECTION

Ask families to continue this game with names at home, using names of other family members. For example, families may use the child's name throughout the day as described above. They may also play silly games with names, such as saying "Are you Mommy? Daddy? Alexander? Oh! You are Alexander! That is you--Alexander!"

Doing It Myself

Purpose: This activity shows the child's desire to become a person separate from her caregiver, and the desire to do things by herself that were done for her before.

Materials: any object or material the child is playing with

Preparation: When the child is playing with a familiar toy, using a spoon, dressing, or doing a familiar activity, notice when the child displays the desire to do it herself by pushing your hand away. The child might also turn away from you to play or take the object with her to another part of the room.

Activity: You might say, "You are ready to do this by yourself!" or "You are getting to be a big girl now!" If the child struggles to continue the activity alone, you can offer to help or step in to assist the child. When the child displays the desire to do an activity without your help, understand that the child is getting ready to do more and more things by herself, and encourage this independence.

Extensions and Variations:

- As you begin an activity that the child might want to do independently, such as putting on a coat, washing hands, or placing puzzle pieces together, ask the child if she wants to do it herself or if she wants you to do it with her.
- When an older, more independent child completes a task by himself, point it out to the child you are teaching and tell her that soon she, too, will be able to do that by herself.
- When the child does a task alone, say, "You did that all by yourself. You did a good job!"

HOME CONNECTION

Encourage families to allow the child to do activities at home independently if the child wishes to. Often this takes longer as the child tries hard to do a task that is easier if it is done for her. Examples are putting on a coat or mittens, eating with a spoon, or washing hands. Although these efforts may be time-consuming and even messy, encourage families to allow the child to do things for herself when she expresses the desire to do so.

Cleaning Up

Purpose: The child learns that there are things that belong to him, and that he can take care of these things. This activity is part of a child's understanding that he is able to control things in his world and be responsible for them.

Materials: any materials you are using during an activity, either at mealtime, during play, or after an activity with music

Preparation: When you finish an activity with the child, do not complete all the clean-up by yourself. Encourage the child to assist you by returning the materials where they belong.

Activity: After completing an activity, ask the children to help place the toys back on the shelves or the musical instruments back in their place (box or basket). Name the items, and direct the children on where to place them, such as saying, "Nina, please put the bells back in the box," or "Josef, please put the puzzle back on its shelf." After snack or meals, ask children to place napkins in the trash bin or place their cups on the sink for washing.

Extensions and Variations:

- Children can have an individual space for their own belongings in the classroom.
- In this space they may wish to keep their coats, shoes, or extra clothes, as well as small mementos of a walk in the park, a small toy from home, or an item to take home to show the family.
- Encourage older children to assist younger ones with putting things away and helping in clean-up activities.

HOME CONNECTION

Encourage families to have the child participate in placing things back where they belong after they have been used. For example, families may have a basket or box just for this child's toys, and encourage him to keep these things in that place. Also, families may encourage the child to assist in small chores, such as placing spoons in the sink, placing books back on the shelf, or setting cups on the table.

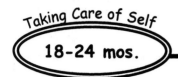
I Can Dress Myself

Purpose: This activity is the beginning of the child's independent dressing and clothes selection.

Materials: clothing the child wears on a typical day

Preparation: Do this activity at the typical time for dressing and undressing. For example, this can be done upon awakening, prior to napping, after the nap, prior to bath time, and prior to bedtime. This activity can also be done each time children get ready to go outside in chilly weather.

Activity: While *undressing* the child, encourage her to help as much as possible. For example, ask her to pull off her shoes, pull off her socks, take off her shirt or undershirt, and the like. When returning from a walk outside, encourage her to remove her mittens, hat, or coat by herself.

While *dressing* the child, encourage her to pull on her own socks, underwear, shirt, or pants. These skills will come later than the skills used in undressing. As you assist the child in getting dressed, show her how you fasten buttons, snaps, or zippers. Praise her for helping you with these, and continue showing her how to do these things until she can do them herself at a later age.

Extensions and Variations:

- Have toys in your classrooms such as large dolls that have clothes that can be taken off and put on.
- Also have toys with buttons, zippers, snaps, or ties that the child can play with and practice on. These can be made if you want to.
- Talk about pulling clothes on and off. "There are three big buttons!" "This coat will keep you warm!" "These pants have elastic in the waist. They are easy to pull on."

HOME CONNECTION

Discuss with families the skills the child is learning at school about dressing and undressing, and ask them to continue these at home. For example, the child may get undressed and ready for a bath at home just as she gets ready for a nap at school. Encourage the family to praise the child's attempts to dress and undress independently.

Comforting Others

Purpose: This activity helps children learn to feel emotions of empathy and comfort. This skill is the beginning of the child's ability to view the world as other people view it, and to understand another person's feelings and point of view. These are important skills for all later peer interaction.

Materials: none

Preparation: This activity can be used when another child is crying, when a nearby adult is upset, or when playing with a doll.

Activity: When the child cries or whimpers because another child near him is upset, comfort him by holding, cuddling, or hugging him and saying something like, "You are upset because Peter is crying. He is your friend and you are sad that he is sad. Let me hug you and make you feel better." Or you may say, "You want Peter to feel better because he is sad. Let's go give him a hug and try to cheer him up. Then he will not feel so sad."

When another child is crying, show the child you are with how to hug, comfort, and pat the back of the crying child.

When playing with a doll, pretend that the doll is hurt or upset, then show the child how to console the doll. Ask the child how the doll might feel now. Take the pretend voice of the doll to thank the child and say that the comforting was successful.

When a child is upset over other people's emotions, calm and comfort him with attention, hugging, and affection.

Extensions and Variations:

- Role-play with the child and a doll, talking for the doll. Talk about how the doll feels sad or hurt.
- Model for the child how to comfort the doll, continuing the conversation with the doll saying how it feels, what it needs to feel better, and other expansions of these feelings.
- Have the doll ask the child, "Do you ever feel sad? What makes you feel better when you feel sad? What do you do when other people you love feel sad? What do you think makes people feel better when they are sad?"

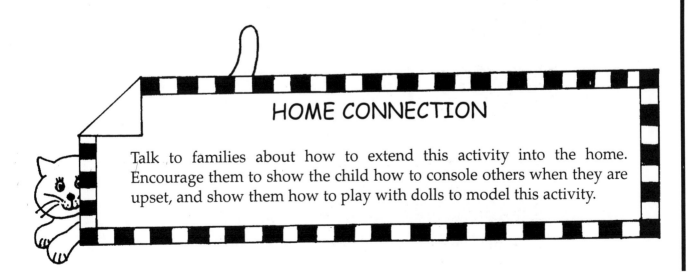

HOME CONNECTION

Talk to families about how to extend this activity into the home. Encourage them to show the child how to console others when they are upset, and show them how to play with dolls to model this activity.

Give Me a Hug

Purpose: This activity supports emotional development by teaching the child that she is capable of expressing closeness and affection. This activity also teaches her that she is able to receive affection in many forms from the people in her world who feel affection for her. When a child receives plentiful affection, she in turn learns how to express these feelings to others.

Materials: doll or soft animal toy

Preparation: This activity may be carried out anytime the child and caregiver are together. This activity can be done when the child is receptive and relaxed, but not when she is intently working on another activity. Select times when the child will not be interrupted from something else.

Activity: Show the child how to affectionately pat the doll or soft animal toy, then show her how to hug and cuddle it. Encourage the child to do the same gently with favorite pets and other children.

Also provide body contact through holding, hugging, and being close to the child as much as possible.

Extensions and Variations:

- When role-playing with dolls or soft toy animals, have them "hug" each other and talk about how they are good friends.
- Have a puppet, soft toy animal, or you yourself give a hug or kiss to the child, and have the child reciprocate.
- When other children join in this activity, encourage them to show affection to each other.

HOME CONNECTION

Encourage families to show affection to their children and to each other. Some families may feel that too much affection will spoil a child. Explain to families that, on the contrary, this affection is a healthy and important part of their child's emotional growth.

Playing in a Small Group

18-24 mos.

Purpose: At this age, children may be aggressive towards each other. They may push, grab toys, pull, or ignore other children. This activity prepares children to play cooperatively when they are older. In this parallel play activity children play near each other, but do not always interact with each other.

Materials: large flat box with a layer of rice or macaroni
paper or plastic cup for each child

Preparation: Select a quiet undisturbed place for play with 2 children together.

Activity: Place the flat box with rice/macaroni on the floor, and help the children play in the material with the paper and plastic cups.

Place the children in an area with 3 or 4 familiar toys. Expect them to watch each other and grab each other's toys. Help each child find a toy of his own to play with.

Extensions and Variations:

- Visit a park or other outdoor area where other children play whenever possible.
- Let the child observe without joining in the play until he wants to join the group.
- When he joins the group, he will probably want to play alongside the other children rather than be a part of the group.

HOME CONNECTION

Encourage the family to invite other children to their home if there are no brothers and sisters for the child to play with. At this age, having only one other child nearby is more tolerable than being with a group of children.

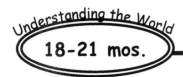

Understanding the World

18-21 mos.

I Can Make That Sound

Purpose: When children reach the age of around 18 to 21 months, they usually start to imitate common environmental sounds from their home and school, such as sounds of pets or farm animals, machines, and sounds from nature. Children may also name an object from its sound rather than by its name, such as saying "Choo-choo" for a train, "Beep-beep" for a car, or "Arf-arf" for a dog. Producing these sounds is an early form of imitation, which occurs prior to the child imitating language and vocal intonation of other people.

Materials: none, other than the sounds that occur naturally in the child's daily activities

Preparation: This activity can be done at any time environmental sounds occur.

Activity: When you are with the child and you hear a typical sound, mention it and imitate the sound. Encourage the child to copy you. For example, when you are near a clock that is ticking, say "Tick-tick-tick," and encourage the child to copy you. Or, when you hear a bell from a bicycle in the street or playground, make a "Ring-ring" sound. This can also be done with the sound of farm animals, a bus, a train whistle, a car horn, and a pet's sounds.

When you and the child are playing with toys such as cars, trucks, or buses, playfully make the sound that the actual object might make. For example, when playing with toy trucks, you might make sounds of "Beep-beep-beep" and the roar of the engine.

When you are playing with musical objects, such as bells or drums, make the sound of the instrument, such as "Thump-thump" for the drum or "Ting-ting" for the bells.

Extensions and Variations:

- When you go on a walk with the child, point out the sounds of the wind in the trees, the rain, thunder, or running water in a small brook.
- Imitate the sounds of the rain or the wind, and encourage the child to copy you.
- During storms or on very windy days, talk about how the sounds are different and imitate them with the child.
- If you have a tape recorder, make a tape of sounds in the environment with the child, then play them back and identify the sound-producing object together.
- When you go on a walk, point out birds and help the child listen to the sounds made by birds. Imitate these sounds.

HOME CONNECTION

In your classroom, have the children talk about the sounds they hear at home but do not hear at school. For example, the children may have family pets that make cat or dog sounds, an infant sibling who cries or laughs in a certain way, or a clock, which makes unusual ticking or chiming sounds. Encourage families to play the noise-making game at home, having the child use the sounds made in the environment to communicate playfully with the family.

Different Textures

Purpose: This activity helps the child learn how to feel various textures and use her hands in more complex ways.

Materials: small tub of water
objects to float: sponges, corks, rubber toys, rocks, small wood pieces, plastic cups, or plastic spoons
rice or other grain
paper
crayons or markers

Preparation: Use 1 or 2 of the objects to float mentioned above. The child or small group of children may be seated at a low table, on the floor, or standing at a table.

Activity: Place a tub of water on a low table and supervise while each child places various objects, such as those suggested above, into the water to see whether they float.

Allow each child to mix the rice and some water, or another grain/small pasta and water to feel the effects.

Place a sheet of paper on a low table with the children seated at the table. Give each child crayons or markers and encourage them to draw, scribble, and make designs.

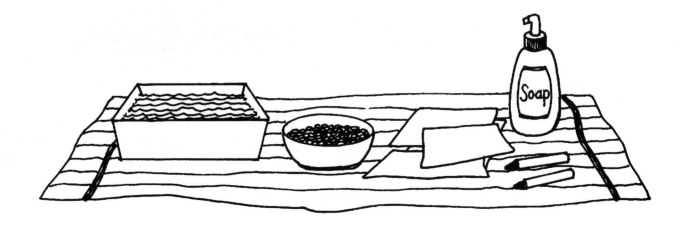

Extensions and Variations:

- Go for a walk with a child and point out the different textures. For example, talk about the bark of a tree, the soft petals of a flower, the crispness of a leaf, or the texture of a fruit or vegetable.
- If there is a sandbox or seashore available, encourage children to play in the sand. If they can go to the seashore, encourage them to look for shells, small pebbles, and other small natural objects on the beach to feel their textures.

HOME CONNECTION

Show families how this type of textural play can easily be done with their children at home. At bath time, children can play with soap suds, shampoo, and water. During cooking, children can play with unused or leftover dough, rice, or pasta. They can also learn about textures in the family garden while playing with the soil, watering the plants, or helping to pick small vegetables such as radishes or carrots.

Painting Time

Purpose: This simple introductory painting activity encourages creativity. Children learn about cause-and-effect relationships when they apply paint to paper. They also learn about the tools a painter uses.

Materials: 2 primary colors of paint in 2 spill-proof containers with tops
large thick paint brushes for toddlers
sponge and small bowl of water for mopping up spills
1 smock per child

Preparation: 1. Children can paint on individual large sheets of paper on a toddler-sized easel or on a very large piece of paper on a table. If painting is done on an easel, make sure the drying line or rack for the paintings is close by.
2. Hang the smock on the easel or place it on the table, near the paint.
3. After the child has put on the smock, bring one color of paint down within his reach. One color of paint is enough to begin with.
4. Children will need a lot of individual help from adults with this activity, so it is best to work with no more than 2 children at one time.

Activity: This activity attracts young children right away. If 2 children want to paint, help them put on smocks. If you are painting on the table, 3 or 4 children may paint. Once children are familiar with painting, it is easier to have a small group. As you put on the child's smock describe how to begin painting by saying, "First we put on the smock, then we paint." Once the smock is on, offer a container of paint, saying, "Here is the red paint."

Observe the child's use of the brush and the strokes. You might need to help the child learn to hold the brush and to add more paint to the brush. Describe the painting strokes by size, length, and color. Encourage the child's attempts and accomplishments. Let the child paint as long as he is interested. If the child wants another color, demonstrate how to put the brush back in the container before offering him another color and brush. Children at this age do not understand that they need to switch brushes for different colors; you will need to explain this and demonstrate.

Children at this age also need help finding individual space, and are likely to paint on another child's work. Some will be happy to paint side by side, but others will want individual space. Observe the children to see who needs to be directed to individual space and who can paint with others. When each child is done, write his name on his paper, help him remove the smock, and wipe his hands.

Extensions and Variations:

- Do a group mural with a large piece of paper. Put a title on it and hang it.
- Add a third color after children have painted with 1 or 2 for a few months.
- Paint boxes (either small or large). Place a large cloth or piece of paper underneath them.
- Hang large sheets of paper on an outside fence so children can paint outdoors.

HOME CONNECTION

Parents can help make smocks or donate old t-shirts for smocks. They can also donate boxes to paint.

I Can Guess What That Is

Purpose: This activity is a precursor to the cognitive ability of object permanence, in which a child knows that an object still exists even though it is not in sight. In this activity, a child learns to (1) recognize objects by feeling them when they are not in view, (2) recognize objects when seen in different contexts, and (3) recognize a class of objects which are similar, such as leaves, blocks, or round beads.

Materials: choose a few of the following: wooden blocks, small plastic toys, animals, or cups, bells, beads, balls, keys, spoons, washcloth, sock
towel
paper bag

Preparation: This is best done in the classroom, either seated on the floor or seated at a low table.

Activity: After you have shown the child 2 or 3 of the objects that are familiar to her, place them under a towel and ask her to place her hands under the towel and feel the objects. Then request that she give you one of the objects without looking at it.

Place 2 or 3 of these objects in a paper bag, and ask the child to give you one of them without looking inside the bag.

Make a small cloth bag with a drawstring top and place different objects in it, one at a time. Ask the child to figure out what is inside without looking. You may include things such as a leaf, a piece of fruit, a sock, a hairbrush, or other familiar things.

Extensions and Variations:

- When you go on a walk with the child, collect things to bring back, such as pebbles, twigs, leaves, or pine cones. Later, have the child identify them in the ways mentioned above.
- During seasonal celebrations include holiday objects in this activity, such as special things with a holiday significance. These may include candles, bells, costumed dolls, or toy animals.
- Place a variety of objects in a basket or box in front of the child. Help her find all of one sort of object, such as all the blocks, all the beads, all the cups, and the like.

HOME CONNECTION

Show families how to use this activity with objects around the home. They might want to have a small box or basket for the child's small objects, and they can add to this and take things away as the child's interests change. With this small box, the child can do the finding, identifying, and sorting/categorizing that are mentioned in this activity.

I Need Your Help

Purpose: This activity furthers the toddler's understanding of the world around him by encouraging him to use adults as sources of information. In this way, the child learns to ask questions that supply answers to his curiosity about the way the world works.

Materials: none, other than materials and experiences the toddler is currently using

Preparation: Be next to the toddler or nearby when he is participating in the activity.

Activity: When the child turns his attention to something new, such as a toy or another person, describe it to him and talk to him about it.

If you notice the toddler losing patience with a task or frustrated with the challenge of using a particular toy, give him information to assist him. For example, if he is putting a 3-to-5-piece puzzle together and the pieces are not fitting, you might say something like, "Try the red one first. Try it another way--there, that's it!"

When a toddler asks about something new, such as a piece of furniture or an appliance, explain how it is used and what purpose it serves. For example, when a child sees a large milk can, explain that the container is used when milk is brought from the cow to the store or house. If he asks about a truck, explain that trucks bring food from where it is grown to other parts of the country.

Express interest in the play activities of the children, saying things like, "You have such nice colors in that painting!" or "You are making the water splash and make noises!"

When you are not sure of an answer, tell the toddler that you are not sure but you can find the answer. For example, if the child asks about the new buildings being built near the school, you might say that these may be offices or apartments for people to live in, but you can find out by asking the people working there.

Extensions and Variations:

- When you are walking in the neighborhood, respond to the child's questions and encourage more questions. For example, if the child asks where a road goes, or why a tree is a certain color, you may explain that there are probably several possible reasons.
- Ask the child what some of the reasons might be.
- On a walk, make a point of stopping by a small market or visiting a produce stand. Encourage the child to ask questions about the things he sees.
- These questions may include where these foods come from, why they come in trucks, how they are used, and why they might be available at some times of the year and not at others.
- When in a small group of different ages, ask some of the older children to give information to the younger ones when they ask. For example, the older ones may be able to name objects or colors.

HOME CONNECTION

Tell parents to expect the child's questions about the world around him, and to encourage these questions. Families may want to select areas of the child's interest and plan to provide more expanded information. For example, if a child is very interested in animals and how they live, the family could visit a farm or a relative's rural home to show the child animals that he would not see at home.

Telling What I Want

Purpose: This activity enlarges the child's understanding of the power of language, and shows her that her attempts at communication result in responses from the people around her. This activity marks the child's ability to create more refined and clear language, which increases her interaction with those around her.

Materials: none

Preparation: None, other than observing and responding to the child's vocalizations and gestures.

Activity: When the child emits unclear sounds to convey her needs, encourage her to point to what she wants. For example, if she is sitting at the table and whines or hits the table, you might say, "Show me what you want. Point to what you would like—is it the juice? The bottle?" When she responds with a gesture or pointing, respond quickly and praise her communication skill, saying "Thank you for telling me what you needed! You wanted the bottle!"

When the child points at or gestures towards something she desires, such as a favorite toy or food, playfully pretend that you need more information until she utters a sound. For example, if she is on your lap and points at a small cup of juice, you might say, "You seem to want something! What could that be? Help me know what it is! Oh! Did you say 'juice'? Here it is--your juice! You told me this is what you wanted!"

When the child uses simple phrases or sounds and gestures, interpret them vocally. For example, when she makes a sound approximating "Milk" and then points to the cup or bottle, say, "Oh! You are asking me for your milk! Do you want your milk? Here it is!"

When you ask the child questions during an activity at school, pause and look at her awaiting a reply. For example, if you are going outside for a walk, you may ask, "Do you want your mittens or no mittens today?" Wait for her reply. If you are giving her a snack, you might ask, "Do you want a small cracker or a cookie?" then wait for her response. Praise her each time she responds to these questions.

Take advantage of mealtimes to get information from the child about what she would like. Rather than present the food and drink all at once, encourage her to ask for what she wants. For example, rather than automatically refilling her milk or juice glass, ask if she wants more. Encourage her to ask for it. Also, encourage her to ask for a fork or spoon by pointing and saying words for it.

Extensions and Variations:

- Offer choices with increasing complexity. For example, rather than giving a choice of water or juice at a meal, let her choose from water, juice, and another drink such as milk.
- When the child is pointing to something new to her, such as a new toy or appliance that she may not know the name of yet, give her the name and encourage her to repeat it after you. For example, if she sees a bicycle for the first time, say, "That is called a bicycle! Bicycle. Can you say it?" She may respond with an approximation, such as "Sickl" or "Bi-ell," but encourage her attempts to say this new word.
- Try a game with a toy telephone in which you have a conversation about what she is doing. This activity encourages speech over gestures because you can pretend you cannot see her on the telephone. Give her a lot of time to get used to talking into the telephone, and respond to her vocalizations with enthusiasm.

HOME CONNECTION

Encourage families to try to understand the child's vocalizations, and let them know which words and sounds she is making at school to signify her wants and desires. Likewise, ask the family what words and sounds she makes at home for communicating her needs. For example, many children use different words at home for food and activities. Communicate with the family about what these words are, so that the child's signals and attempts to make herself understood are clear.

Singing

Purpose: Listening to songs is a rich learning activity for the child, because he enjoys the rhythms, repetition, and varied intonations. When the child sings along with words in a song, he is learning intonation and imitation skills as well as having fun. Although the child's first experiences with songs are simple attempts to talk and repeat what he is hearing, his singing becomes clearer with time and his words can be understood. The child often develops a few songs that he loves to sing repeatedly, and in this way the words become words he uses outside of the singing itself.

Materials: simple tube of rolled paper

Preparation: None, other than simple daily routine activities during which you can sing.

Activity: Sing simple rhythmic songs with short verses. Examples may be short 2- or 3-line songs or nursery rhymes. If a song can be sung with a familiar story, the learning experience is enriched for the child.

When you do simple routines, such as feeding, bathing, cleaning up, or going to bed, sing simple songs, which are either familiar to the child or songs that you make up in a silly way for that activity.

Hum or whistle tunes and add nonsense syllables playfully. When the child sings a playful song, imitate him. Sing together and dance or make simple hand gestures.

Use a roll of paper, such as a tube, and show him how sounds change when sung through this tube. Sing songs into this tube, and take turns back and forth making sounds and singing songs through it.

When you sing a familiar song with him, stop and let him fill in the words at times. The child's words may not be the same ones as those in the song, but encourage him to participate and reciprocate.

Extensions and Variations:

- When you are singing with the child, use empty cans, sticks, or pots to tap out the rhythm.
- Make simple shakers by putting a few beans in a can and sealing it shut. Shake these in rhythm to the songs you are singing.
- Make up songs about upcoming events to assist the child in anticipating the event and learning words for it. For example, when the child is going to visit relatives for a family vacation or a holiday, invent silly songs about where the child will be going, the things he will see, the people who will be there, and the foods that will be eaten.
- This activity is fun in a small group of 2 or 3 children.

HOME CONNECTION

Encourage families to visit your program and watch these music games with their children. Encourage families to continue this playful activity at home, making up songs about the family routines of the day. They might want to include verses about family activities, such as visiting the farm, riding in the car, making favorite foods, and celebrating the holidays.

I Know Names of Things

Purpose: This activity assists the child with naming pictures, which are symbols of familiar objects. Although the child will have already learned to point to a picture of a familiar object or person when the caregiver asks her to, naming requires expanded understanding of symbolic representation. In other words, this skill demonstrates the child's understanding that words and pictures are symbolic of events or objects. This ability is an important component of early literacy and later reading skills.

Materials: pictures of familiar objects from storybooks, magazines, photograph albums, or any other source

Preparation: Arrange for quiet time with a child and the pictures.

Activity: When you see a picture of an object familiar to the child, ask, "What is this?" then give the child time to respond.

If you see several pictures on a page, ask the child where one is. For example, if the page has pictures of food, you might ask, "Where is the apple?" or "Where is the bread?" Later, ask the child what it is when you point to the picture.

When the child points to a picture of an object she does not know, enthusiastically encourage her curiosity and explain, "That fruit is called a cherry. They are sometimes here in the spring after the weather is warmer!" Make the child a book with pictures of her favorite familiar people and objects, then go through this book often, asking "Who is that?" or "What is this called?"

Extensions and Variations:

- Expand upon what the child says when she names an object or person. For example, if the child says "Grandmother," you might add, "Yes, that is Grandmother wearing her red sweater at her house."
- Likewise, when the child says "Mittens," you might add, "Yes, these are warm wool mittens. We wear them when the weather is cold and it snows."
- When you make a book for the child of her favorite and familiar things, first use pictures of objects as they appear in real life, such as a photo or picture of the object.
- Next, encourage the child to find a colored illustration of the object. For example, if the child has a favorite soft animal toy and enjoys naming the animal toy in her book, show her a page in another children's book with a similar soft toy and ask her to find it.
- Later, see if the child can identify a black and white picture or drawing of the same object.
- Once the child has mastered that identification, see if she can locate simple drawings of familiar things, such as a car, house, or animal.

HOME CONNECTION

Encourage families to use books made for the child at your program, books that they have made at home, family photos, and children's storybooks to ask the child to name 2 or 3 familiar objects. Communicate with the family about which words the child knows and can say upon recognition of the objects, so these can be repeated at home.

My First Sentences

Purpose: The child begins using sentences to express meaning. Up until now the child has used a few words to express wishes and needs, but at this stage he learns to place names of things (nouns) with names of actions (verbs) to describe events. For example, the child might say "Mama go" when his mother leaves him at the school, or he might say "Yuri eat" when he is having a snack. These brief sentences form the foundation for expression of more complex action descriptions later.

Materials: none, other than those present when the child is playing or involved in an activity

Preparation: None.

Activity: While looking at a simple picture book or storybook, ask the child to describe what is happening. For example, you might point to a picture and say, "What is happening?" The child may respond with "Car goes," "Child cries," "Boy runs," "Horse eats," or "Kitty sleeps."

When the toddler is involved in an activity, ask him what he is doing. He may respond, "Josef eating," "Alexander jumping," or "Max wash hands."

When you are doing simple activities with a toddler, tell him what is being done. For example, you might say, "Eva is hugging the doll," "Anna is turning pages in the book," or "Julia is resting."

Extensions and Variations:

- When you are on a walk and see machines or construction, explain what is happening, such as saying, "They are building a new road. They are making the ground flat for the road now."

- You might add something like, "They are building a building for people to live in. The building will have rooms for each family like your houses. They are putting the walls up for the rooms now."

- While on a walk outside, encourage the children to tell you what other people are doing. They may say, "Man waters garden," "Lady gets mail," "Man does shopping," or "Boy rides bicycle."

HOME CONNECTION

Share with families the words and phrases the child is using, and ask them what words and phrases they may have heard at home. Encourage them to tell the child often what each person in the family is doing during activities, such as "Big sister sews," "Daddy shaves," "Grandmother gets the eggs," or "Aunt Nina is reading." Suggest that they ask the toddler to tell them what he is doing. He may say, "Josef eating now" or "Peter washing."

Telling You How I Feel

Purpose: The child learns to express emotions, recognize feelings, and describe events that go on around her. In this activity, the child develops the beginning structure with which to form language and give shape to the experiences in the world around her.

Materials: none other than those the child is involved in at any time

Preparation: None, except to be with the child or in close proximity.

Activity: When showing a child a simple storybook, explain how the children or people in the story might be feeling, such as saying, "He was really surprised to see the puppy there!" or "She felt sad because her milk had spilled."

When the child is feeling a simple emotion, tell her how she might be feeling. "You are happy to be playing in the water!" "You enjoy it when Grandmother visits us and plays with you!" "You are sad when Mommy goes back to the house while you are at school." "You feel angry when you need to wait your turn."

When the child is experiencing feelings such as those stated above, ask her to tell you how she feels in words.

When the child is playing with different objects or is engaged in different activities, ask her what she is doing and encourage her to elaborate. What will it look like? Where will she put it when it is done? What is fun about it?

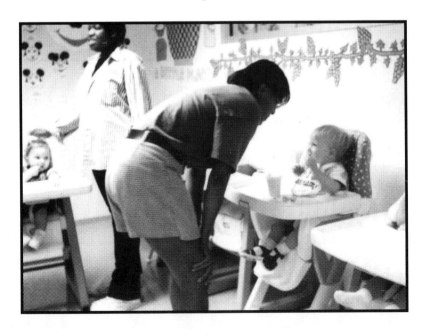

Extensions and Variations:

- When a toddler briefly states what is happening in a couple of words, expand this by stating it more fully.
- For example, if the child says, "Ball go fast," you might respond by saying, "Yes, the ball rolls very fast. You are strong to roll it that fast!"
- Or, if the child says "Soup gone," you might respond by saying, "Yes, you ate your bowl of soup. Soup is warm on a cold day, isn't it? Would you like a little more soup?"
- When the child uses expressions such as noises rather than words, expand them with the words themselves.
- For example, if the child says "Arf-arf go fast," you might respond, "Yes, the dog is outside now. He will come back in later."
- Likewise, if the child says "Choo-choo come," you might respond with "Yes, the train is coming to the station. It will arrive soon!"

HOME CONNECTION

Share with parents ways to expand and clarify the words the child uses, and how to label emotions and experiences. Communicate to families the words the child is using, and the new concepts which may be emerging soon. For example, if you are going on walks in the neighborhood during early spring, let families know that they may hear their child saying the new words she learned during these walks, such as *muddy, path, sticks, leaves,* or *flower.*

I Love to Climb Things

Purpose: The child learns social skills, releases energy, explores new ways to climb and move, and experiences different ways that his body can move through space. These activities teach the child balance, coordination, and physical mastery of large muscle movement.

Materials: open space in the classroom
classroom "gyms" with steps and slides
toddler tricycles
sandboxes
bars the children can swing from

Preparation: Be sure that the environment for this play is open, free of objects that may hurt a child, has a soft surface on the floor, and allows space for running and tumbling.

Activity: Play with the child in a variety of ways, such as taking him for piggy-back rides, holding him up to touch the ceiling, and helping him to do somersaults and stand on his head. He can also hang from a bar or tree branch, jump on a mattress or small trampoline, and chase other children.

Children love moving on small tricycles, rolling toys such as trucks, lying on flat toys with wheels, and playing on small stairs followed by small slides they can slide down.

Using music, encourage children to move like their favorite animals. For example, using slow music, have them move like an elephant, or using faster music, have them trot like a horse. Have them stretch like a cat, or curl into a ball like a sleeping dog.

Place a hammock in a corner of the play area either inside or outside the classroom. Show children how to use the hammock, and also how to gently rock each other in this hammock.

Have a quiet time before and after these activities to help transition the children into and out of these activities calmly. For example, you may precede these with story time, a singing circle, an art activity, or the like, and they may be followed by a similar slow activity such as painting, listening to music, or taking a nap.

Extensions and Variations:

- When you go outside, either to a playground or to the school's play area, encourage these activities.
- Encourage children to explore trees and help them pull themselves up or hang from a branch.
- If you have access to a playground, teach children how to swing, how to climb equipment built for that purpose, and how to use other available outdoor equipment.
- In mixed age groups, be sure that each child is participating in a way that is safe and appropriate for his age.
- Allow different activities for younger and older children, separating the more active children from the children who do not walk yet.

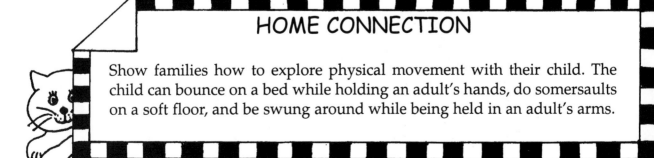

HOME CONNECTION

Show families how to explore physical movement with their child. The child can bounce on a bed while holding an adult's hands, do somersaults on a soft floor, and be swung around while being held in an adult's arms.

Moving All Over

Purpose: The child learns the physical feeling of moving her body in various directions against gravity. This is called proprioceptive movement. It is the foundation for more refined movements as the child matures, and for development of later complex balance and motor coordination.

Materials: child-sized stairs and slides
large cushions
slippery fabric
tunnel made of chairs and a sheet or blanket

Preparation: Be in an open space with the child-sized materials listed above.

Activity: Help the child learn how to climb down stairs by creeping backwards on her hands and feet. As she comes down each step, place her knees and feet on the steps below to instruct her how to do this safely.

Later, the child will come down the stairs facing forwards by holding your hand and stepping down each step. During this time, the child will place both feet on the same step prior to stepping down to the next step.

Lift the child into the air and say something like, "We are moving up!" or make up a song about it. When you put her down again, say "We are going down now." Make this a game, moving her slowly up and down while telling her what you are doing, such as "We are going up, up, up! Here we are--so high! Now we will come down, down, down!" Repeat as often as you wish.

Provide chances for the child to slide down a slide. If you do not have a slide, place large cushions so that they form a low slide, then place slippery fabric over them. Hold onto the child as she slides down this slide. Use the words "up" and "down" as you do this.

Create a tunnel for the child to crawl through using chairs and a sheet or blanket. Make this a fun obstacle course as the child crawls through the tunnel, then climbs and goes down the slide, then returns to the tunnel.

Extensions and Variations:

- Extend this idea of the obstacle course by including a long flat piece of wood for the child to step over, another chair to climb under, another large pile of cushions to climb over, or a larger tunnel under a table for the child to go through.
- Flying a kite with a child is a wonderful activity. It provides opportunities for the child to run and pull, and creates a sense of accomplishment.

HOME CONNECTION

Show families the types of physical movements you are doing with the children, and encourage them to replicate these at home. For example, if the family farms, they may want to include the child in gathering eggs, searching high and low for them in the barn. If the family has large animals, they may want the child to have a brief ride on the back of a horse while being held securely by an adult. These kinds of activities may also include climbing a ladder or sliding down a wet bank of a nearby body of water. All activities need to be done with sufficient supervision from adults.

Moving Through a Maze

Purpose: Children move through a maze constructed with various obstacles and equipment. The maze offers practice for children's large motor abilities. They problem-solve as they decide how to move through the different-sized openings.

Materials:
walking boards (4 cm x 30 cm x 1 m to 2 m)
tumbling mats
carpet squares
large blocks
sheets or blankets
tunnels

Preparation:
1. Construct the maze with large motor equipment in the classroom. For example, large motor equipment might include large wooden blocks or a slide. Make tunnels out of sheets and blankets draped over furniture. You may also purchase children's large tunnel toys. Include passageways, balance beams, and different textures such as boards or carpet squares to walk on.
2. Build the maze so it requires different types of movement such as crawling, walking over a block, walking on a balance beam, and jumping over a mat.
3. Build the maze with more than one entrance and exit and more than one way to move through it.
4. Make sure the maze is safe and items will not be pulled over or tip.
5. Use this activity throughout the day and continue to vary it for as long as the children are interested.
6. Consider beginning with 2 children in the maze and 2 watching.

Activity: Observe the children discovering the maze. At first, the maze will be very attractive to all of the children. Be prepared to limit large groups in the beginning. If more than 4 want to try it, tell them that they will have a turn after the first 4. Encourage them to watch the others as they appear and disappear. Talk about the maze as they experience it. "Josef, you are moving across the carpet. Now you are at the wall. What will you do?" Encourage children to move through tunnels by putting yourself at the other end. Try not to hurry the children. Let them explore until they are finished.

Extensions and Variations:

- Crawling infants like tunnels. They have difficulty waiting for a turn; consider offering them a tunnel nearby with 2 chairs and a blanket.
- Children might help you plan the maze and construct it.
- Add to the maze a little every other day.
- Take the maze apart slowly, a little every day when you are finished.
- Construct a maze outdoors.

HOME CONNECTION

Invite families in to see the maze. Children will find it funny if their parents try to do the maze.

Big Movements, Little Movements

Purpose: The child explores both the large muscle movement (gross motor) of jumping and running, as well as small muscle (fine motor) movement of using her hands to play with objects. This activity teaches the child to coordinate both large and small, and fast and slow movement.

Materials: musical instruments
colored scarves or pieces of bright cloth
paper streamers
balance beam
balls of various sizes

Preparation: Find enough open space in which the child can move freely.

Activity: Play music of different tempos and encourage children to move to the music and dance. Have the children continue to move to the music while holding a scarf, a paper streamer, or a ribbon.

Clap and stamp your feet in simple slow and fast rhythms. Encourage the children to imitate them. Then clap in patterns and encourage the child to imitate you, such as 2 fast, pause, 2 fast and the like.

Play simple games, such as songs with hand gestures, clapping, swaying, foot stomping, and have the children imitate your actions.

Jump with the toddler as you hold her hands.

Make a balance beam using a flat board and have the child walk on it while holding your hand. Encourage her to jump off while still holding your hand, then encourage her to walk on it alone.

Play games with balls by rolling the ball back and forth while you are sitting on the floor. Begin with a very large ball, then gradually do this with smaller and smaller balls. If there are no balls like this, you can make balls by crumpling paper.

Play games of chase and encourage the child to follow you.

Extensions and Variations:

- Introduce a game of "Follow the Leader," in which you move while encouraging the child to imitate your actions. For example, you might have her imitate you while you run, crawl, do a somersault, roll sideways, walk backwards, or turn in a circle.
- When you are outside, encourage children to play freely in a park or other open area. They may want to play "Follow the Leader" in a large meadow, roll down a hill, roll balls back and forth, or play musical games while sitting in a circle.

HOME CONNECTION

Bring families in to your program as often as possible to see these games and activities, and encourage them to do some of these activities when the family is outdoors. For example, if the family has outdoor picnics or barbecues, encourage them to have a place where the children can play.

Chapter Five:

The Two-Year-Old

What Is the Two-Year-Old Child Like?

The two-year-old explores everything. This child moves quickly and constantly. She is beginning to master her body and feelings, and is learning to be independent in every way. She can dress and feed herself. She loves to pretend, although in less complicated ways than the older child. She wants to learn to play with peers, but needs a lot of adult support to do this.

Here are a few more characteristics of the two-year-old:

- Likes to practice doing things by herself
- Can pour from a small pitcher and fasten clothes with snaps, large buttons, and zippers
- Understands her own perspective, and only a little of what others feel and think
- Experiences sudden mood changes
- Is interested in peers and can play a simple game with adult help
- Learns about her effect on others by grabbing, hitting, and pushing
- Understands and responds to adult requests
- Can name most familiar things
- Can match and sort by shape and color
- Uses 300-1,000 words, but cannot put feelings into words
- Lacks coordination and may spill or tip things over
- Can pedal a small bike.

When planning the classroom, consider that the two-year-old is similar to both the toddler and preschooler. Like the toddler, this child plays quickly with what interests her at the moment. Self-paced activities are best. Two-year-olds have a limited understanding of time. For them ten minutes seems very long. Group times should be limited. Most of the time, two-year-olds learn best with free choice or routine activities.

A Picture of Many Faces

Purpose: This activity is a gluing or pasting experience in which the child makes a picture using cut-out pictures of children's faces. The child uses faces with different hair and eye colors, of different races, and with and without glasses. The experience helps the two-year-old comment on similarities and differences and develop a sense of "who I am." The child practices using small muscles and explores creativity.

Materials: pictures of children or faces (different skin color, glasses, etc.) from used magazines
old shower curtain to cover table
paper to place the pictures on
damp cloth
glue or paste
small wooden sticks to spread glue or paste

Preparation:
1. Place the curtain or other covering on the table to catch any spilled glue.
2. Place the pictures on the table either in small baskets or on the table.
3. Up to 4 children with 1 adult is best for this activity.

Activity: Let each child choose a piece of paper on which to glue her pictures. Place glue or paste in a small container with small sticks near the child. Let the children choose from many cut-out faces on the table. Observe and respond to the children's comments about the faces. They may comment on eye or hair color, or ask questions about skin color. Answer these questions clearly and simply. For example, "Yes, this girl's skin is light and this girl's skin is darker." Or, "These are glasses, she wears them to see better. Your dad wears glasses, too." Help children with the glue. Some will get a lot on their hands and be unable to pick up more pictures. Have a wet cloth nearby to wipe children's hands as they work.

Extensions and Variations:

- Use pictures of girls and boys to help children think about gender.
- Use pictures of babies. Children at this age are very interested in babies.
- Some children will be fascinated by the glue or paste. Consider other activities using these materials, such as torn paper collage, making simple books, and making paste with children.
- Make a group picture using a large piece of paper

Paste for Toddlers

80 ml or 1/3 cup wheat flour (not self-rising)
2 large spoons sugar
250 ml or 1 cup of water

Mix flour and sugar in sauce pan. Add water slowly, stirring constantly. Stir until lumps are gone. Cook over low heat until the mixture is clear, continuing to stir constantly. Let the paste cool to room temperature before using. Store in a covered container for several weeks.

HOME CONNECTION

Be prepared for the children to make negative comments about the faces. They may be noticing differences or reacting to stereotypes. Consider talking about stereotypes in a parent meeting. Parents could discuss how they feel about differences between people of different races and religious backgrounds.

I Am Happy, Sad, Scared, and Mad

Purpose: The child learns words to express feelings. The caregiver shows her feelings and tells the child the words that go with them. Then, the child practices expressing the feelings.

Materials: none

Preparation: This activity can be done with 1 to 4 children.

Activity: Introduce this activity to a child or small group by saying you are going to make happy and sad faces. Ask a child to show you a happy face. Show the child your happy face. Repeat this game with different feelings of sad, scared, and mad. If the child does not yet know how to make a face when you ask, make the face yourself as a model. Or, ask another child to try to make the face. You might say, "This is how I look when I am scared. Can you make a face like mine?" Keep playing this game until the children tire of it and ask to do something else.

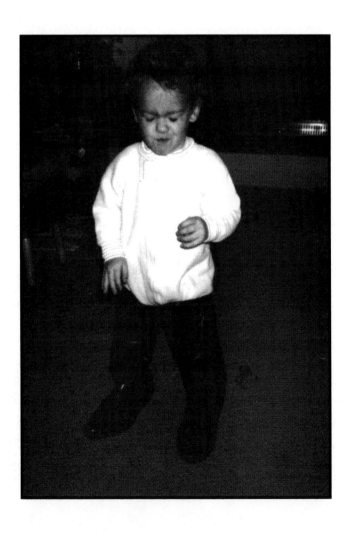

Extensions and Variations:

- Ask younger children to name the feeling on your face. (See "My Feelings.")
- Use a mirror. Ask the child to look in the mirror and make the faces.
- Make up a story using these feelings of happy, sad, scared, and mad. Ask the children to show the feelings in the story.
- When the children can make the faces, add voices. See if the children can make their voices and faces express the feelings of happy and sad.

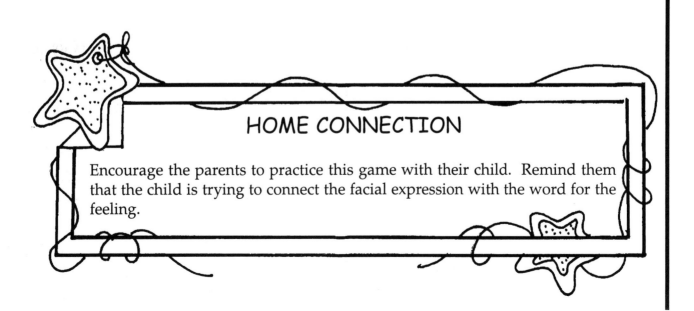

HOME CONNECTION

Encourage the parents to practice this game with their child. Remind them that the child is trying to connect the facial expression with the word for the feeling.

Matching Socks

Purpose: Matching familiar things such as socks is an important step in learning to get dressed. This activity teaches children how to put together like objects and promotes the ability to sort objects.

Materials: 4 to 6 pairs of different-colored socks
basket to hold socks

Preparation: 1. Mix up the socks in the basket.
2. Place the basket on a small table or on the floor.
3. This activity can involve up to 3 children.

Activity: Observe the child who chooses the activity. Watch how the child explores the socks. Some children like to try the socks on. Encourage the child's work by saying, "Anna, you can put 2 green socks together. You are matching the socks." If the child has not yet labeled colors, introduce them. Name the color of the sock the child is holding. "Anna, you are holding a black sock in this hand. Can you find another black sock?" Help her find the matching sock if she is unsure. Try another pair. Continue encouraging the child to match as many as interested. If the child wants to continue after all are matched, mix the socks up and begin again. Two-year-olds really like to mix the socks again.

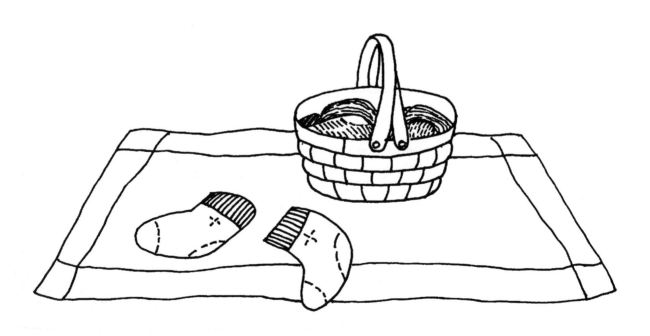

Extensions and Variations:

- For the younger child, mix the child's familiar pair of socks with another pair. The child will enjoy sorting the socks and then putting them on.
- Sort other clothing such as mittens, t-shirts, or shoes.
- Use small and large socks. See if the child can sort by size. With older children, ask them to sort by color and size.
- Put the basket in the pretend play area. Children can practice sorting the laundry as they play house.
- Make pairs of socks or mittens out of paper. Cover with plastic and keep in a shoe box. The child can use clothespins to put the pairs together. This game can be left with other manipulative toys for children to explore further.

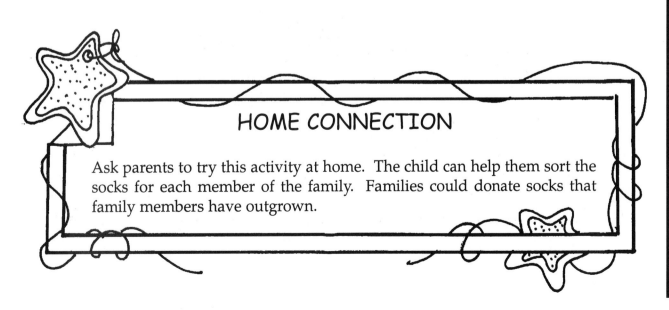

HOME CONNECTION

Ask parents to try this activity at home. The child can help them sort the socks for each member of the family. Families could donate socks that family members have outgrown.

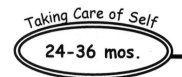

Dress Up

Purpose: Two-year-olds practice dressing up for cold weather. They also learn about the connection between warm clothing and cold weather. The activity is good for children's use of their imaginations.

Materials: winter clothing—hats, ear muffs, jackets, boots, scarves, warm socks
mirror
old camera

Preparation: 1. Assemble the clothes. Hang these on hooks in the pretend play area for children to explore freely. Or, use the clothes as a special activity and place them in a large basket in the middle of the room.
2. This activity is good for up to 4 children.

Activity: Encourage the toddlers to dress up for the cold weather. Try on some clothes yourself to show them. Suggest that the children look in the mirror. You might use the camera to take their picture. Talk with the children about the different items of clothing. Point out the name of the item, its color, and its texture.

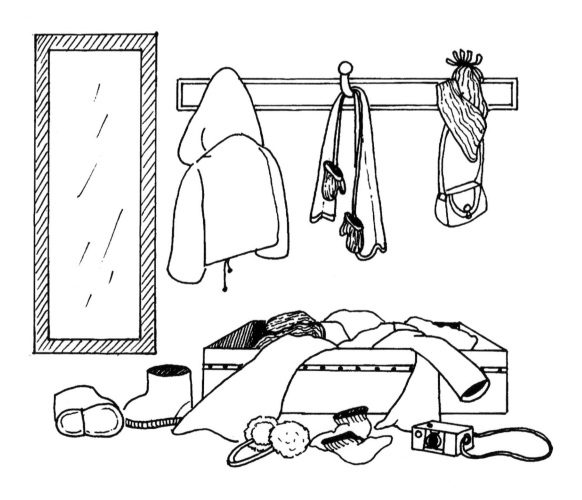

Extensions and Variations:

- Collect pictures of people dressed up in winter clothing. Look at the pictures and point out the names of the items of clothing.
- Have a "warm hat day" when everyone wears a winter hat from home.
- Look for children's books about winter and read these. A good example is *The Snowy Day* by E. J. Keats.
- Make a group mural by cutting and pasting pictures of people in winter clothing from old magazines and catalogues.

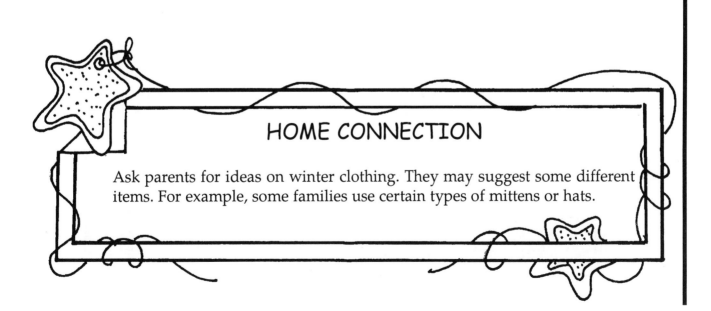

HOME CONNECTION

Ask parents for ideas on winter clothing. They may suggest some different items. For example, some families use certain types of mittens or hats.

Washing Up

Purpose: The children help wash the furniture and toys. They learn about washing and practice valuable skills using their hands and eyes. Most of all, they take pride in helping to take care of their classroom.

Materials: dish tub
mild dish soap
sponges
small cloths
smocks
towels or small drying rack

Preparation: 1. Collect some toys to wash.
2. Put a small amount of water in a dish tub. The dish tub can be on the floor, on a small table, or in the sand and water table.
3. Put a small amount of dish soap on the sponges and cloths and in the water.
4. This activity works well with up to 2 children per dish tub.

Activity: Tell the children that they can help wash toys. Help them put on smocks. Put toys in the dish tubs to wash. Talk with the two-year-olds about how to clean dirty things. When finished, place the items on the rack to dry or dry them with a towel.

Extensions and Variations:

- Over the next few days, wash toys in the room by adding different toys to the tub each day. Let the children suggest toys to wash.
- Two-year-olds like to wash furniture. Let them help wash chairs (a favorite). If the weather is warm, this is a good activity for outdoors.
- Wash the doll clothes. Hang up a clothesline and let the children hang the clothes with clothespins.
- Use spray bottles with water to wash outside. Two-year-olds enjoy learning how to make these work.

HOME CONNECTION

Ask each family how they clean their home. Try to use the same cleaning tools (scrub brushes, cloths) in the classroom. Find out about the family routine for cleaning. Is it in the morning or afternoon? Do they do laundry at home or outside the home? Do they sing while they clean? Try to imitate these family routines and talk about them while the children are cleaning in the classroom.

Using Tools

Purpose: The child practices self-help skills with real tools for eating and self care. This activity promotes using the child's senses and small motor coordination.

Materials: small tubs
small objects such as blocks, pretend fruits and vegetables
variety of tools such as:
    spatula
    tongs (small and large)
    tablespoon
    tweezers
    spoons with holes
    needle-nose pliers

Preparation: 1. Place the objects in the small tubs. Start with similar tools, for example— spoons and spatulas. These are the easiest to use. Use the tongs, tweezers, and pliers in another tub or when children are ready. This way the children use a similar action with different tools.
2. This activity can occur during choice time in the sensory table.
3. Two children can work at a tub and up to 6 can work at the sensory table.

Activity: Observe the children as they explore the objects and the tools. They may want to use their hands to find objects and then use the spoons to move the objects. Encourage them and show them how to move the objects with the tools. Talk with them about what else the tools can move, for example different foods. When children are ready, introduce more complex tools such as tongs, tweezers, and pliers.

Extensions and Variations:

• You can have 2 tubs and place the objects in one. Encourage the child to move the objects from one tub to another using the tools.
• Add a small amount of sand. The child can remove the objects from the sand with the tool.
• Use spoons outside with a pile of small rocks that the children have gathered. They can practice moving the rocks from one pile to another.

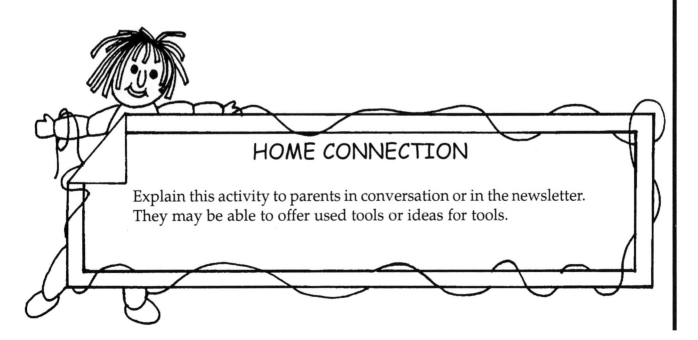

HOME CONNECTION

Explain this activity to parents in conversation or in the newsletter. They may be able to offer used tools or ideas for tools.

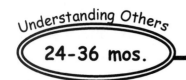

24-36 mos.

Celebrating Holidays

Purpose: The children talk about different holiday celebrations and learn about individual differences.

Materials: none

Preparation:
1. Find out how families celebrate birthdays.
2. This is a good group conversation for up to 6 children. You might talk during a routine, such as lunch, when children are in a group or during a short, group time.

Activity: Talk with the children briefly about a celebration such as a birthday, a wedding, or a religious event. Let children give you ideas about how they celebrate the holiday, for example, the special foods, clothes, or activities of people in their families.

Extensions and Variations:

- Collect a variety of baking items, such as pastry tins, whisks, bowls, measuring spoons, empty spice containers, aprons, and hot pads. Encourage the children to bake celebration cakes for each other. Model the use of the tools. Put these in the pretend play area or on a table for a special activity.
- Share your holiday celebrations with the children. They love to hear about you.
- Find and hang posters or pictures of holiday celebrations.

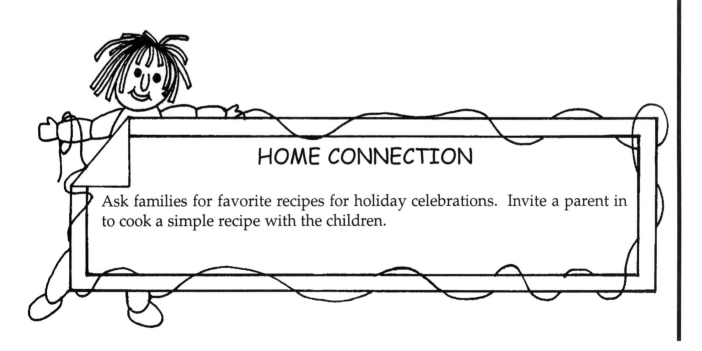

HOME CONNECTION

Ask families for favorite recipes for holiday celebrations. Invite a parent in to cook a simple recipe with the children.

Teddy Bear Picnic

Purpose: The children take teddy bears on a picnic and learn about warm feelings of celebration on this special day to honor each child's favorite bear. This activity takes more than a day with planning. Children help plan the place of the picnic and what to eat. They learn to plan ahead and anticipate the picnic.

Materials: teddy bear for each child from the classroom or home
blanket to sit on
food for the picnic (jam sandwiches or finger foods, such as carrots or fruit)

Preparation:
1. Send a note home to let parents know about the picnic. Invite the child's favorite stuffed animal, doll, or teddy bear to the picnic.
2. Children may not have a favorite bear and prefer to bring a stuffed toy from the classroom. Assemble these and a few extras for the picnic.
3. Decide with the children where the picnic will be outside and have an inside location in case of bad weather.
4. This is a large group activity. Plan on having enough adults, including parent volunteers, present.

Activity: On the day of the picnic, the children can help prepare the food and get the blanket. Talk with each child about her special bear or animal, the name, color, eyes, etc. Politely ask the child if you can hold her bear. This provides an example for the children when asking to hold another child's bear. Gather together the food, and blanket. Take the children, bears, and picnic supplies outdoors to the picnic place.

Eat the snack and sing the songs about teddy bears during the picnic.

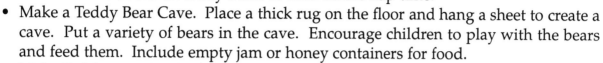

Extensions and Variations:

- Find or make books on teddy bears to read before nap time.
- Make a Teddy Bear Cave. Place a thick rug on the floor and hang a sheet to create a cave. Put a variety of bears in the cave. Encourage children to play with the bears and feed them. Include empty jam or honey containers for food.
- Make Teddy Bear Sandwiches. Children can spread jam on bread with dull knives and put two pieces of bread together to make sandwiches. Cut bear shapes out of the bread with cookie cutters to make the sandwiches look like a teddy bear.

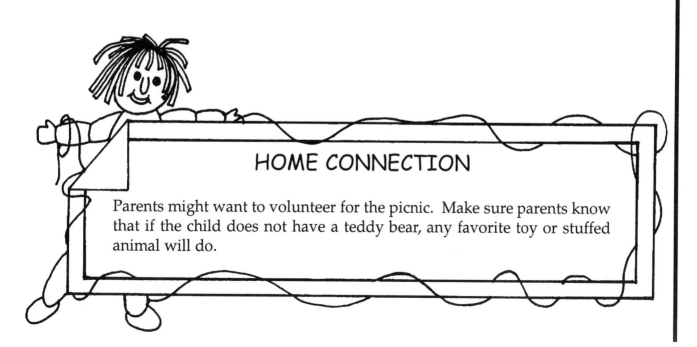

HOME CONNECTION

Parents might want to volunteer for the picnic. Make sure parents know that if the child does not have a teddy bear, any favorite toy or stuffed animal will do.

Making Gifts

Purpose: The children make gifts for each other by putting classroom toys in boxes and wrapping them. They learn about feelings of giving and practice small motor skills when wrapping the gifts. Wrapping gifts also promotes creativity.

Materials: boxes (send a note to parents to ask for help collecting boxes)
used wrapping paper (ask parents to help supply this)
tape (cut small pieces for the children to use)
used ribbon or string

Preparation: 1. Assemble all of the materials.
2. This activity can be done on a small table.
3. Plan on up to 4 children at a time.

Activity: Observe the children exploring the boxes. Suggest to a child that he can wrap a toy for a friend to play with. Start by hiding a toy in the box, putting the cover on it, and presenting it to a child. The children may want to play this way before wrapping. When a child is ready to wrap, help choose the wrapping paper and tape it on the box. Remind him to place the toy inside before wrapping. When the box is wrapped, encourage him to give it to another child as a present. You might say, "Peter, here is a present for you." Let them know the recipient can open the present. Children will enjoy rewrapping the box with other toys as presents. Some children will find it difficult to give up the gift they wrapped. Encourage them to share, but accept that not every child is able to share.

Suggest that the children wrap gifts to take home to their families.

Extensions and Variations:

- Younger children can hide toys in boxes and find them.
- Decorate boxes with markers and crayons instead of wrapping them.
- Use a large box and have a group work together to cover it. This project may take more than a day.
- Some children are fascinated with tape. Consider a taping activity, where the child can practice using tape by sticking small pieces of tape on a sheet of paper. To save tape, cut small pieces. To help the child use the tape, stick the pieces to the edge of a bowl.

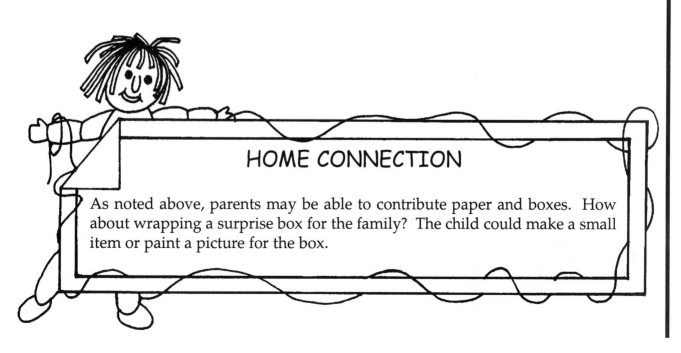

HOME CONNECTION

As noted above, parents may be able to contribute paper and boxes. How about wrapping a surprise box for the family? The child could make a small item or paint a picture for the box.

Train Friends

Purpose: The children pretend to be train cars. This activity promotes social interaction and creative movement. The children also practice large muscle skills.

Materials: none

Preparation:
1. Read a book about trains to find out what the children know. Do they know about engines, cabooses, train whistles, and train sounds?
2. This activity works best with small groups of 2 or 3 children.

Activity: Suggest to the children that they be "train friends." You could model this with one child. Have the child be the caboose and you be the engine. The child holds on to your waist, you shout "All aboard!" and move around the room making train sounds. Help children pair up as train friends. Make train noises and pretend to blow the whistle as you move. After a few minutes, come to a stop at the "station." Have the cabooses and engines switch places and repeat the activity.

Consider pairing more active two-year-olds with more tentative children so they learn to work together.

Extensions and Variations:

- Play recorded music of train songs or a clear rhythm as you move.
- As children become more familiar with the activity, add another person or train car.
- This activity works well outside.
- Read books about trains and consider visiting a train if one is nearby.

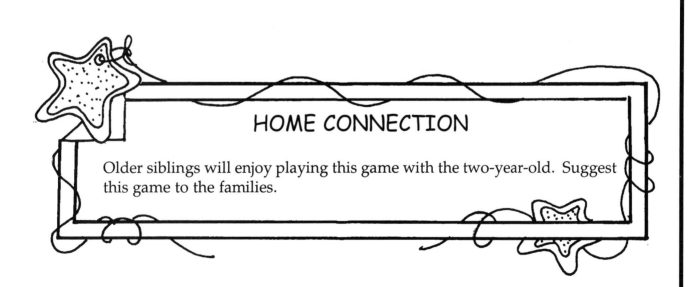

HOME CONNECTION

Older siblings will enjoy playing this game with the two-year-old. Suggest this game to the families.

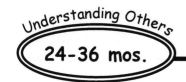

Toddler Slumber Party

Purpose: The children pretend to be sleeping at each other's home. This activity promotes social interactions and use of their imaginations.

Materials:
old slippers
old clock
small blankets
stars and moons shapes on string
t-shirts (adult-sized for pretend pajamas)
quiet music

Preparation:
1. Assemble the materials in the pretend play area.
2. Hang the moon and stars from the ceiling or put them on a window.
3. Small groups of up to 4 work best.

Activity: Observe the children using the materials in the pretend play area. When they appear ready to try something, suggest a slumber party. Explain to them that a slumber party is when friends or relatives sleep at your home. Encourage the children to put on their pretend pajamas by putting on a t-shirt. Make a place to sleep and cover yourself with a small blanket. Nap or exercise mats can be added for a pretend bed.

Play quiet music. Encourage the children to pretend to sleep. They can cover each other and the dolls with the blankets. Read bedtime stories or sing lullabies. The children may want to wake up and then repeat this activity.

Extensions and Variations:

- Use dolls and stuffed animals for the slumber party.
- Talk about their own bedtime routines so children are more aware of each other.

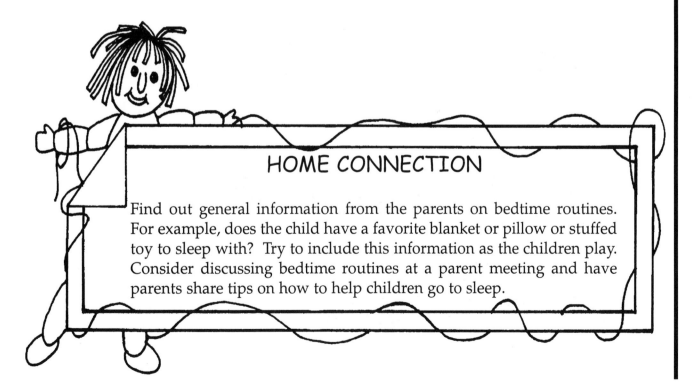

HOME CONNECTION

Find out general information from the parents on bedtime routines. For example, does the child have a favorite blanket or pillow or stuffed toy to sleep with? Try to include this information as the children play. Consider discussing bedtime routines at a parent meeting and have parents share tips on how to help children go to sleep.

Making Playdough

Purpose: Playing with playdough is a wonderful activity that encourages development in many ways. Two-year-olds are ready to help make the playdough. They can learn about cause and effect as ingredients are mixed together. They learn about properties of ingredients and how they change by adding other dry or wet ingredients. Making playdough offers experience with math concepts of measuring. When playing with the finished product, the child uses creativity and problem solving.

Materials:
4 parts flour	1 large, 1 medium, and 1 small bowl
1 part salt	measuring cups
1 part water (approximately)	measuring spoons
1 large spoonful of vegetable oil	5 large spoons
smocks	

Preparation:
1. Assemble the ingredients.
2. Choose a place where the surface can be easily cleaned, such as the sand and water table.
3. Measure the salt and flour in the small and medium bowls.
4. Measure the water in the measuring cup.
5. This activity works well for up to 4 children and 1 adult.

Activity: This activity works well during choice time. Prepare the area. As children approach, tell them that you are making playdough. Ask up to 4 children if they would like to help. If more want to help, they can watch until there is room. This is often a popular activity and everyone wants to help.

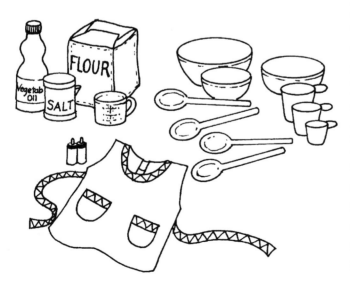

Place the large bowl on the table. Put the salt, flour and water near you on the table. The children can help pour the dry ingredients one at a time into the bowl. Add the vegetable oil to the water while they observe. Then a child can pour the water and oil mixture into the large bowl. Hand out large spoons to everyone including yourself. Let each child take a turn mixing. Make sure you mix a little at the beginning. This ensures that the ingredients get mixed and you can demonstrate how to use the spoon.

Add water if the mixture is dry. Mix until the dough forms a ball. Once the dough is well-mixed (after about 5 minutes) tell the children you will knead it with your large hands to finish it. Knead about 5 minutes. The dough should be smooth and not too sticky. If sticky, add more flour. When finished, give each child a small amount to play with. More children may play once the playdough is mixed.

As you are mixing, observe the children to see what they say. Ask them what happens when different ingredients are added. The children may notice how the dough feels different as ingredients are mixed. Some children like to taste the playdough. Encourage them to play with it instead.

Extensions and Variations:

- The caregiver can also make the playdough in advance.
- Add color with food coloring in the water or dry paint in the flour. Let the children choose the color.
- Try other recipes for playdough with the children. Talk about the different ways to make playdough.
- Add rolling pins (small wooden cylinders) and cookie cutters.
- Make bread to practice kneading with the children.

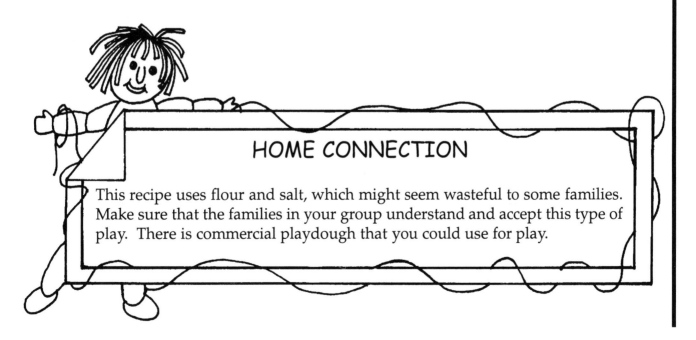

HOME CONNECTION

This recipe uses flour and salt, which might seem wasteful to some families. Make sure that the families in your group understand and accept this type of play. There is commercial playdough that you could use for play.

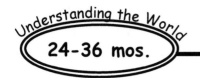

Torn Paper Collage

Purpose: The child tears paper and pastes the pieces. This activity develops creativity and gives the child experience using eye-hand coordination. A group project promotes social awareness.

Materials: colored paper scraps or old magazine pictures
paste and small wooden sticks
crayons
large piece of paper to paste on

Preparation: 1. Choose a small table to work on, and tape the large piece of paper to it.
2. Prepare paste by placing small amounts on 2 or 3 small pieces of paper.
3. Place paper scraps within children's reach, and spread these out on the table.
4. This activity works well with up to 4 children during free play.

Activity: Tell the children you are making a picture out of small pieces of paper. Show them how to tear paper. Explain they can tear different sizes of paper. As they tear, talk about the sounds they hear. Point out the different colors of paper they are using. Show them how to paste the small pieces on the larger piece of paper. Some children will want to add crayon coloring to the collage.

Some children will be interested in tearing the paper but not interested in pasting. They can tear pieces to place in a small pile for others to use. Tearing paper feels satisfying and is good for expressing feelings. Some two-year-olds may be more interested in pasting. Let them paste lots of pictures. Help them figure out the amount of paste required for different sizes of torn paper. This can be a group project. Use the crayon to write children's names near their work.

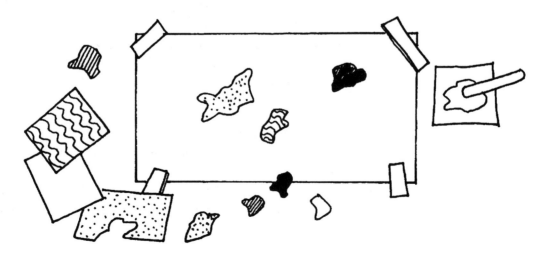

Extensions and Variations:

- Children with difficulty seeing or using small motor coordination will enjoy tearing.
- Use different types of paper such as aluminum foil, wallpaper, and tissue paper. The textures feel and sound different when being torn.
- Encourage the older children to tear simple shapes, such as circles, triangles, and squares.

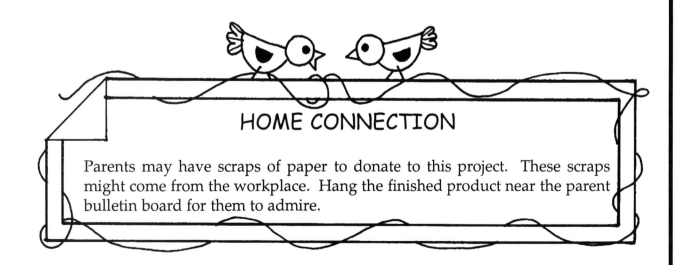

HOME CONNECTION

Parents may have scraps of paper to donate to this project. These scraps might come from the workplace. Hang the finished product near the parent bulletin board for them to admire.

Collecting Natural Treasures

Purpose: The child collects and identifies items from outdoors and learns to classify natural things. The child learns about the environment through her senses as she looks, touches, and smells the different things. The child uses small motor skills as she collects the objects.

Materials: leaves
sticks
rocks
assorted items from outside
buckets, large basket, or dish tub to collect items
small sacks or baskets for children to sort items

Preparation: 1. Choose a place to collect natural items such as the playground, a nearby park or outdoor area with trees or bushes.
2. Do this activity as a group with an adult for 4 children. Eight children total is enough.

Activity: This activity works best if the whole group collects items and places them in the dish tub or large basket. Then, you can sort the items into smaller sacks or baskets either right away or when you return to the playground. Let the children help gather items from the ground. Place the items in the large tub or basket. Talk about the items they collect. You may need to explain the difference between a natural and made item. Include only natural things and put the trash in a small sack.

When you have filled the large tub or basket, it is time to sort. Take the basket back to the classroom or playground. Talk about the colors, textures, and size of the items they collected. Point out hard, smooth, and soft surfaces. You can sort simply by putting rocks together, sticks or twigs together, and leaves together. Or, sort by color or size.

Extensions and Variations:

- Have each child fill an individual sack. Write the child's name on the sack before you begin. When you return to the playground, have each child empty the sack and talk about the natural treasures. If the children are willing, place the items in a large tub or basket for all to examine.
- Take the sensory tub outside for all to examine. See what children can add from the playground.
- Collect rocks in sacks and paint these when you return. This painting can be done inside or outside.
- The children can sort the items by color, size, or weight.

HOME CONNECTION

Talk with parents about the treasures. Parents sometimes wonder why their two-year-old wants to pick up things from the ground. Explain to the parents that the child is curious and that it is easy to turn the child's habit into a learning activity. They can help the child sort the trash from the natural treasures.

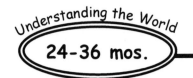
Printing Circles

Purpose: The child uses different circular objects and paint to print circles. This activity encourages creativity and is good practice for small motor skills. The child becomes familiar with different sizes of circles.

Materials: variety of circular objects: lids from containers, tops for spray cans, small plastic containers, and paper towel rolls
small shallow tray for the paint
large sheet of paper for printing
smocks

Preparation:
1. Assemble the circular objects.
2. Place the objects in a basket or dish tub for the children to explore.
3. Mix 2 colors of paint.
4. Pour paint into small shallow trays or pie plates.
5. Add 2 or 3 circular objects to each color of paint.
6. Cut the large piece of paper into a circle, tape it to the table. This is for printing on.
7. This activity works well with up to 4 children at a time.

Activity: Tell the children that you are making circles. Demonstrate how to put the circular object in paint and make a print on the paper. Encourage the child to print with the different objects. Talk to the child about the objects, colors, and printing while working.

Some children will be fascinated by the prints. Some will be interested in the paint. They will touch it and make a print mark with their fingers. Talk with them about the marks they make. Encourage them to make a circle with their fingertips!

Extensions and Variations:

• Use only 2 to 3 items for children who have difficulty seeing. Use large objects for children who have difficulty with eye-hand coordination.
• Think about printing with other shapes such as squares or triangles. Search for materials to use for these shapes. You might include some washable small blocks.
• Match the color of the paint to the color of the objects for printing.

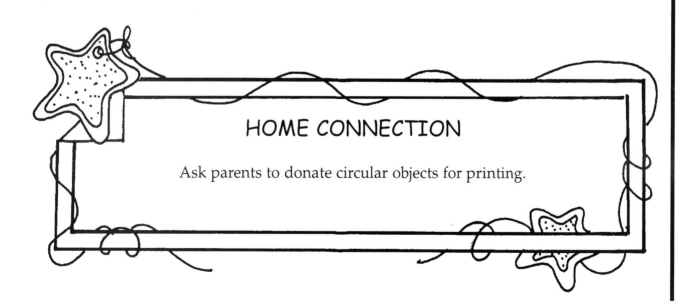

HOME CONNECTION

Ask parents to donate circular objects for printing.

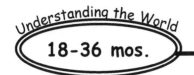

Birds in the Nest

Purpose: The child places pictures of birds in empty nests and uses his visual and matching skills. This activity helps eye-hand coordination.

Materials: paper of different colors for birds and nests
clear plastic to cover
scissors
utility knife
large sheet of cardboard
small plastic bag
glue
double-faced tape

Preparation: 1. Cut 2 to 5 birds out of thick paper.
2. Cut a nest for each bird out of the same color or design of paper.
3. Cover the birds and nests with clear plastic.
4. Attach the nests to the cardboard with glue. Leave the top edge open.
5. Store the birds in the small plastic bag and tape to the back of the cardboard.
6. Do this activity with up to 2 children at a time during a choice time.

Activity: Show the child how to slide the bird into the nest. Encourage the child to have the bird return home to the nest of the same color. Some children will explore sliding the birds in and out of the nest before matching the colors. Observe the child as he explores and talk about how the bird goes in and sits on the nest. Share your interest in birds with the child. Children are fascinated by birds and love to hear how they fly and build their nests.

Extensions and Variations:

- For a child who has difficulty with visual discrimination, use only 2 birds. Make the birds and nests out of fabric. The child can match the texture by touch.
- Make a large bird and a large nest and a small bird and a small nest. The child can match the birds and nests by size.
- Go on a bird walk. See what types of birds you can find and look for nests.
- Collect pictures of different birds and their nests. Make these into a large picture or a small book.
- Make nests with the children. These can be made out of natural materials such as sticks, leaves, and mud. They can also be made out of torn paper and paste.

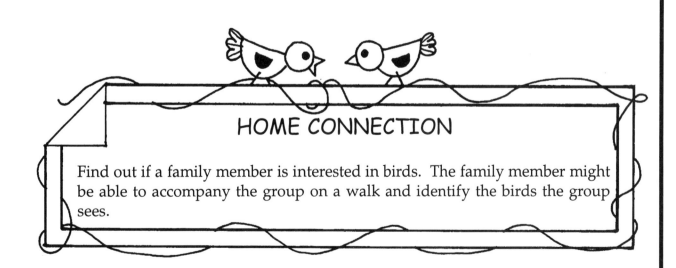

HOME CONNECTION

Find out if a family member is interested in birds. The family member might be able to accompany the group on a walk and identify the birds the group sees.

Story Time

Purpose: Children listen to a story before lunch or nap time. The story can help children calm down. This group time activity is different from spontaneous reading during play time. The activity introduces the children to books and prepares them for later reading.

Materials: books for children
simple songs or rhymes in which children can use their hands and fingers

Preparation:
1. Read stories in the book area of the room. Include a small rug and pillows to make the area comfortable. For this activity and other group times, you might add small carpet squares, one for each child. This helps the children find a place to sit.
2. Read books to children in small groups. Have 2 caregivers so each one is with 4 to 6 children.
3. Plan on reading 2 books. Choose a book yourself and have a child choose a book each day. Select a book topic that is interesting or related to the children's experience, for example the birth of a sibling, a visit from relatives, or a favorite animal.

Activity: After washing hands for lunch or preparing for a nap, sit down with a small group. Encourage the children to sit. Start with a song to get their attention. Songs in which children can use their hands and fingers, also called "finger plays," are the best for this age, since they allow children to move around. Introduce the finger play before doing it. "Marina wanted us to sing a song about a train." Introduce the books after the finger play by saying, "We have 2 books. This one is (book title). We'll read it first." Children will want to talk about the book. Help them take turns talking. If children ask for other finger plays, try to do these. If you are reading before nap time, make sure you move slowly and choose songs that are relaxing for the children.

The Two-Year-Old

Extensions and Variations:

- Younger children like to sit on your lap or lean on you as you read.
- Older children may also like flannel board stories.
- Make sure the children who have difficulty seeing or hearing are close to you.

HOME CONNECTION

List the books you are reading in the newsletter. Parents might enjoy knowing about these. You could also include finger plays in the newsletter for parents to sing at home.

211

Binoculars

Purpose: The caregiver makes binoculars with the child's help. Playing with binoculars encourages the child to use language. The child experiences sights and sounds and the use of binoculars focuses the child's senses.

Materials: cardboard tubes—empty toilet tissue or paper towel rolls
masking tape or clear tape
yarn or string

Preparation:
1. Tape 2 short tubes together side by side to make a pair of binoculars. One or 2 children could help.
2. Make enough pairs for half of the children
3. This activity works well with 4 to 6 children.

Activity: If you do this activity inside, sit down in a comfortable area where children can see you. They will come over to look and see what you have. Ask the children who approach if they are interested in using the binoculars. Demonstrate how to look through them and how to report what you see. "I see the pillows and Alexander reading a book." Children will walk around the room looking through the binoculars. Ask them what they see. Repeat what they say. If the binoculars fall apart, have the two-year-olds help repair them with tape.

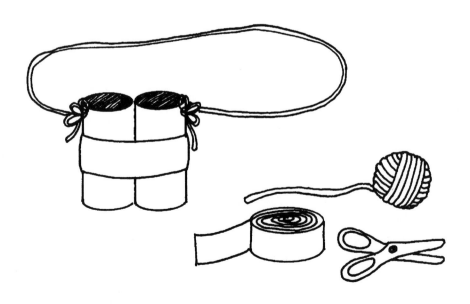

Extensions and Variations:

- For younger children, use a single tube. It will not fall apart.
- For older children put colored plastic at the end of the tubes, and have them look at each other.
- Take the binoculars outside and look at nature: bird watching, examining clouds, or whatever catches the interest of the children.
- Use a long tube as a telescope or spyglass.
- Use these tubes for examining sounds. Put a long tube to the ear and listen.

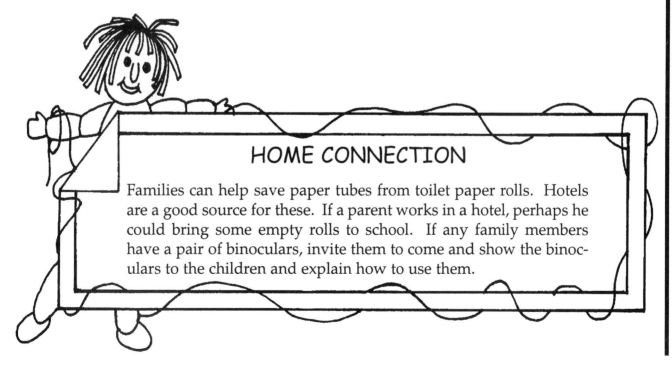

HOME CONNECTION

Families can help save paper tubes from toilet paper rolls. Hotels are a good source for these. If a parent works in a hotel, perhaps he could bring some empty rolls to school. If any family members have a pair of binoculars, invite them to come and show the binoculars to the children and explain how to use them.

24-36 mos.

Toy Telephones

Purpose: Children help make and then "talk" on toy telephones. This activity stimulates language use. Children pretend to be talking on the telephone, which encourages their creativity and ideas about adult roles. Talking on the telephone is also a social activity and encourages social interaction.

Materials: round juice containers or empty toilet paper rolls
paper to cover the juice container
masking tape or clear tape
markers or crayons

Preparation:
1. Make a telephone by taping the end of the paper roll or juice container. Two or 3 children can help you tape.
2. Cover the container with paper.
3. Write numbers 0-9 on the roll, beginning with 0 on the roll.
4. This activity works well during play when children can choose whether to participate. Work with up to 4 children per adult.

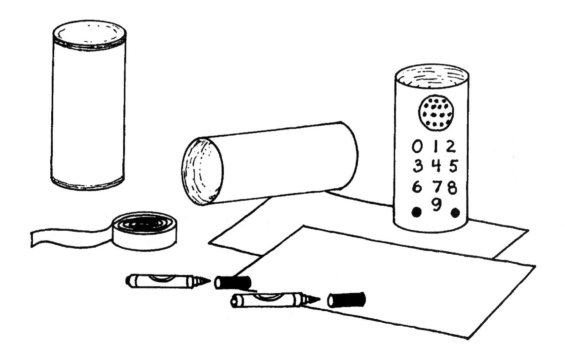

214

Activity: Select an area where children can both make and play with the telephones. If you place yourself near the dramatic play area, children might use these in playing house. As a child approaches you, tell him you have made toy telephones. Demonstrate how to talk on the telephone by pretending to call the child up. Hand him another telephone so you both can talk. As more children approach, help them to begin conversations and keep them going. The conversations will be short. At first, children will rely on you to think of what to say. Suggest they call another child who is nearby and hand a telephone to that child. Or, suggest they call their mother or another family member.

Extensions and Variations:

- For younger children, have toy telephones or used telephones for them to explore. Some children will enjoy touching the telephone or carrying it around.
- For older children, add a variety of telephones to the dramatic play area. They will enjoy having conversations with you and other people.
- Play the telephone game with older children. Sit with 3 or 4 children in a circle. Whisper a simple phrase in the ear of the child next to you. Have that child whisper the phrase to the next child. The last person tells the group what was whispered. Be ready for anything. Children often say whatever is on their minds. Accept what they say.

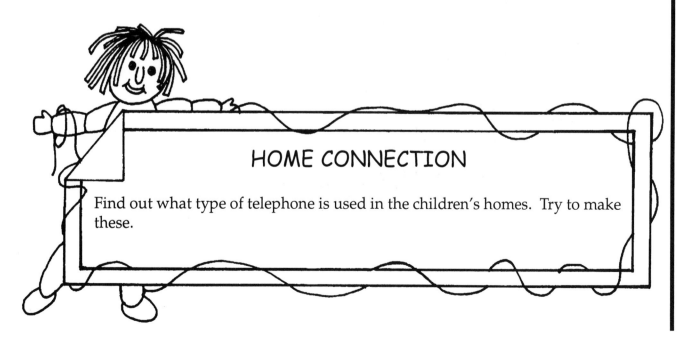

HOME CONNECTION

Find out what type of telephone is used in the children's homes. Try to make these.

Taking a Trip

Purpose: The child packs a suitcase or backpack and pretends to take a trip. This activity encourages expressive language and stimulates dramatic play. Children learn vocabulary related to packing.

Materials: 1 small suitcase or small backpack per child
1 or more of the following: shirts, hats, pairs of shoes, small animals or dolls

Preparation: Assemble the materials. The dramatic play center is a good place to do this activity. Or, place the objects on open shelves. Up to 4 children could do this activity, depending on the number of materials.

Activity: Observe the child's interest in the materials. Decide when the child is ready to play. You might begin by offering some ideas. Suggest that the child pack to go to visit a relative. When she is packing make some comments such as, "Julia, do you need a hat? What do you have packed?" Once the child is packed, you might ask, "Are you ready to leave on the trip?" She may take the suitcase to another part of the room. If not, suggest a place. When she arrives, the child might unpack the suitcase. Promote language by asking her to label different items. The child may want to repack and go back, then unpack. Continue for as long as she seems interested. Some children will concentrate on packing and unpacking with minimal language interaction. Accept their limited explanations and answers. They may be more interested in the function of packing.

Extensions and Variations:

- Younger children will be content to put things in and take them out of the suitcase. They might like to use the suitcase latch.
- Older children might like to discuss adding other real props for traveling.
- Play a suitcase game with the older children, using imaginary objects. This begins with "I packed my grandmother's suitcase and in it I put a toothbrush." The next child says the same thing and adds a new item. "I packed my grandmother's suitcase and in it I put a toothbrush and a _____." This is a good game for improving memory and vocabulary.

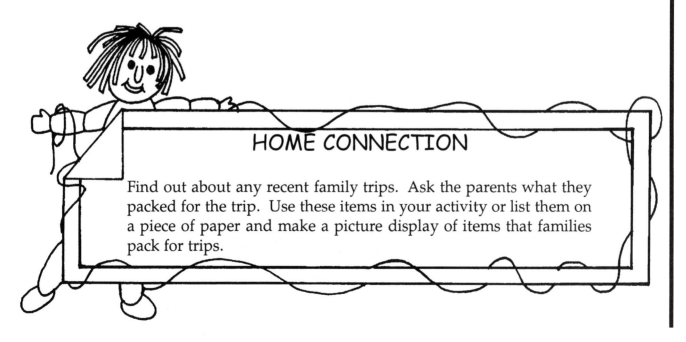

HOME CONNECTION

Find out about any recent family trips. Ask the parents what they packed for the trip. Use these items in your activity or list them on a piece of paper and make a picture display of items that families pack for trips.

Puzzles

Purpose: Children play with teacher-made puzzles. Puzzles help them practice eye-hand coordination and build skills for reading and writing. Children learn to see similarities and differences which is important for reading later on. Doing puzzles brings a feeling of confidence and satisfaction. Two-year-olds enjoy puzzles with 3 or 4 pieces, although some will appreciate a simple puzzle of 2 pieces.

Materials: heavy cardboard
small wooden pieces for knobs
sharp knife or single-edged razor blade
glue
empty boxes of child's favorite cereal or crackers

Preparation:
1. Shape puzzles are made by first tracing a shape on the heavy piece of cardboard. Make a 2-piece puzzle and others with 3 or 4 shapes. Cut out the shape with the knife. Try not to use the tools around children. Make the edges as smooth as possible.
2. Picture puzzles are made from pictures on boxes of cereal, crackers, or labels from canned food. Make a simple puzzle, using the front of the box, by cutting the box in 2 parts down the middle. If using labels, glue the label to heavy cardboard and then cut it in 2 or more pieces.
3. To make the puzzles simpler for younger children or children with difficulty seeing, glue small wooden knobs to each piece. This makes the pieces easier to see and manipulate.
4. Put the puzzles on the shelves with other manipulatives and work with children in small groups as they choose the puzzles. Or, put them on a small table for a small group activity with 2 to 4 children.

Activity: Observe the children to see what they are doing with the puzzle. Some will approach, look, and touch. Invite them to put the puzzle together. With some children you will need to demonstrate and they will imitate. Begin with a 2-piece puzzle and when they successfully complete this, offer a puzzle with 3 pieces. Others who have experience need only hints from you and not a demonstration. Observe their strategies. You might suggest, for example, that they turn the puzzle piece so it fits. Encourage them by saying, "Josef, you put the circle puzzle together."

Extensions and Variations:

- Younger children will explore the puzzle pieces by dumping them on the floor. You can point out the pictures and name objects as they manipulate the pieces.
- For older children and children who enjoy this activity, continue to add more pieces to the puzzles.

HOME CONNECTION

Make puzzles in a parent meeting. Parents can make one for the classroom and one to take home.

Making Raindrops

Purpose: Children use droppers and water and pretend to make raindrops. They practice their fine motor skills. This activity also helps a child understand cause and effect.

Materials: eyedroppers
basters
nasal syringes
dish tub or sand and water table
water

Preparation:
1. Assemble the droppers and syringes.
2. This activity can be done in the sensory tub or in dish tubs on a low table. Fill tubs with water.
3. Have enough droppers for up to 6 children. Plan on 2 or 3 children per dish tub and up to 6 at the sensory table. Make sure you have more droppers than children.

Activity: Explain to the children that they can make raindrops with these tools. Show them how to squeeze the bulb and empty the eyedropper and other tools. Encourage them to experiment with the different droppers. Some children will find this difficult and only try for a short while. Others will practice for a long time. Some will be interested in the effect of the drop on the water's surface. Talk with them about this and find out what interests them.

Extensions and Variations:

• Younger children and children with visual challenges can use large basters.
• Older children might enjoy using small eyedroppers with colored water in small clear plastic containers. They can move the water from one container to another and watch the colors blend and change.
• Use eyedroppers with colored water on light paper such as coffee filters. Children can make designs. You can hang these as a mobile from the ceiling in the nap area or for young babies to observe.
• Go on a walk outside and observe raindrops falling in puddles.

HOME CONNECTION

If a family member works in a place where droppers can be found, she might be able to help supply some for this activity. Encourage families to let the child use the baster at home to play with water in a small bowl or dish tub.

Feeding Birds

Purpose: The child makes a bird feeder and learns about birds and their food. Fine motor skills and eye-hand coordination are encouraged with the stringing activity.

Materials: yarn or string
round oat cereal
old circular crackers or pretzels
scissors
tape

Preparation:
1. Cut the string or yarn into approximate 15 cm (6") lengths.
2. Tie a knot at one end. Wrap a piece of tape around the other end to make stringing easier.
3. This activity should be done on a small table with a small group of up to 6 children at one time.

TAPE

Activity: As children approach the table, explain that they will be making feeders for the birds. Show each child how to string the cereal. Encourage the child to string the food. If the oat cereal is difficult to string, suggest trying with the pretzels or other food with a large hole. Some children will want to use both cereal and pretzels. Encourage the children not to eat the food, but to save it for the birds. When a child says he is finished, tie the ends to make a loop. Hang the feeders outside on tree branches. Watch the birds eat from a classroom window, if possible.

Extensions and Variations:

• Older children could think about what else to feed birds. Experiment with their suggestions and try stringing these items.

• Hang a bird feeder near the classroom and put birdseed in it. Watch it daily. Ask the children, "What birds go to the feeder?"

• Go outside for bird watching. Have as many adults along as possible. As you walk, look for birds. Watch what the birds are doing. For example, they might be sitting on the ground, flying in the sky, searching for food, resting in trees, or drinking from puddles.

HOME CONNECTION

Find out if there are parents who watch birds and can tell you more about them. Ask parents to come along on the bird watch or to see the feeders.

Exercising

Purpose: The children exercise with a doll as a demonstration. They increase their body awareness and exercise large muscles. This activity is important for developing good health habits.

Materials: cloth doll with arms and legs that move easily

Preparation: You may do this with a small group of up to 4 children or with a large group and some more adults helping.

Activity: Gather the children in a small or large group and suggest exercising. Introduce the doll and activity. "My doll is named Johanna. Johanna likes to move her body. Let's do what Johanna does with her body." Move the doll and describe the movement. "See Johanna move her arms. Can you do this?" Some favorite movements are nodding the doll's head, jumping in place, touching your head and toes, turning in a circle and stretching to touch the ceiling. Comment on the children's movements. "Katrina is nodding her head. Up and down her head goes. Nina is turning around in a circle." When the children have exercised for 5 to 10 minutes, help them calm down before stopping. Use slower motions or have them sit on the floor and do smaller motions, such as clapping or touching their toes. Some children may want to continue. Have more dolls so that they can practice demonstrating the movements.

Extensions and Variations:

- Exercise to music.
- Younger children will join in and enjoy imitating the older children.
- Have the children exercise while moving streamers and bells.

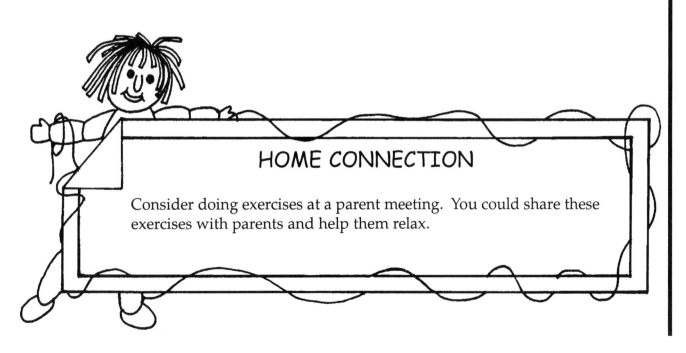

HOME CONNECTION

Consider doing exercises at a parent meeting. You could share these exercises with parents and help them relax.

Bottle Bowling

Purpose: Children use bottles for a bowling game. By rolling the ball they practice large motor skills and eye-hand coordination. This game also helps them understand cause and effect as the ball hits the bottles and knocks them down. When children play together, they learn how to cooperate and take turns.

Materials: 6 to 8 two-liter plastic soda bottles
small amount of sand
large or heavy ball

Preparation: 1. Put sand in the bottom of the bottles. Replace the caps.
2. Set the bottles up in 2 rows.
3. Have an area where children can roll the ball without interruptions, for example, a secluded area in the classroom or the hallway.
4. This activity works well with 2 children. A child can set up the bottles while the other rolls the ball. Use another ball and 2 rows of 4 bottles for more children.

Activity: Show the children who are interested how to roll the ball and knock over the bottles. Help 2 children play by suggesting one can set up the bottles while another rolls. They then switch places. Talk about what happens when the ball hits the bottle and bottles hit other bottles. Ask what kind of sound it makes.

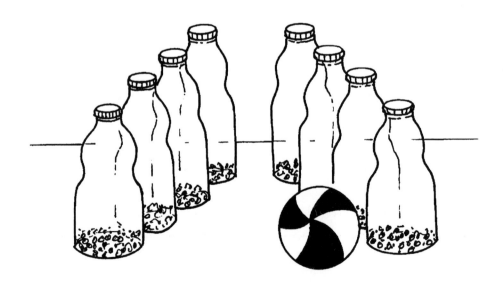

Extensions and Variations:

• Younger children will enjoy rolling the ball. They also like to chase the ball. Use a large soft ball.

• Try this activity outside and talk about how the ball rolls on different surfaces.

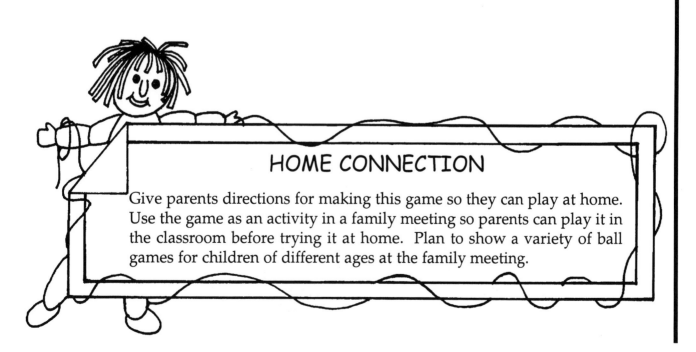

HOME CONNECTION

Give parents directions for making this game so they can play at home. Use the game as an activity in a family meeting so parents can play it in the classroom before trying it at home. Plan to show a variety of ball games for children of different ages at the family meeting.

Scrub Painting

Purpose: Children use fine motor and large motor skills as they scrub while painting. The painting is an opportunity for creative expression.

Materials:
toothbrushes
shallow container
1 or 2 colors of paint
paper
dish detergent
smocks

Preparation:
1. Collect 2 to 4 old toothbrushes for painting.
2. Mix paint and add a small amount of dish detergent for bubbles and easy clean up.
3. Pour the paint into a shallow container.
4. Dip toothbrush in paint and then paint on the paper.
5. This activity is done in the art or sensory area with up to 4 children at once.

Activity: As children come to see what the activity is, explain that you will be scrub painting with the toothbrushes. Offer the child a piece of paper on which to paint and help the child put on the smock. Show the child how to paint with the brush by moving it back and forth or side to side on the paper. Talk to the child while she paints. "Anna, you are moving the brush back and forth. What a beautiful design!" The dish detergent may make bubbles in the paint as the child moves the brush. Ask the child, "What are those? Where did they come from?"

The child may want to use the second color of paint. Let her continue until she says she is done.

Extensions and Variations:

*   Use larger brushes (scrub brushes) for the younger child and 1 color of paint. Use big sheets of paper to encourage large arm movements.
*   A large piece of paper is good for a group mural.
*   Use scrub brushes and buckets of water with detergent to wash furniture such as chairs. This is a good outside activity.

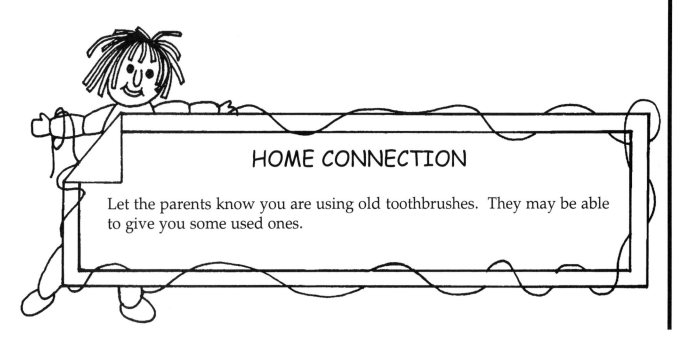

HOME CONNECTION

Let the parents know you are using old toothbrushes. They may be able to give you some used ones.

Chapter Six:

Using Themes with Toddlers and Twos

Planning With Themes: Toddlers and Two-Year-Olds

Planning with themes is one way to integrate learning experiences. Theme-based planning for toddlers and two-year-olds:

- Connects individual activities
- Involves the senses
- Is simpler than for children older than two years
- Is based upon the children's actual experiences.

Themes are a way to offer children of this age experiences that are holistic and include all areas of development: emotional, social, language, intellectual and physical. The child has the opportunity to use a variety of materials and centers in the classroom.

Why Use Themes?

Most of the learning for toddlers and two-year-olds is process-oriented. The child moves quickly from one experience to another, and her activity appears to be unrelated. Careful observation by the caregiver provides clues about how the child connects experiences. For example, a toddler dresses a doll in the dramatic play area and pretends to wash his doll in the sink. The caregiver observes this and understands that the child is very interested in taking care of babies. She wonders if more of the children share this interest. After observing other children's play and conversations, the caregiver sees that they are also interested in babies, although in different ways. One child is interested in baby toys, another in feeding babies. One way of responding to this interest is to plan a series of learning activities around the theme of babies. Planning this theme offers all of the children more choices for learning about babies. The variety of experiences leads to integrated learning for the children.

The Planning Process

The interests of the children are central to the selection of the theme. The first step is to observe the children. While not all children have the same interests, they do have common experiences. Some interests are known to the caregiver in advance, and some will appear during the year. Most children are interested in food, so planning a food theme is appropriate. Sometimes a trip to the grocery store as part of a food theme suggests another theme. For example, children discover worms on the street and are fascinated. The caregiver notes this interest and observes further to find out more. What fascinates them? Is it the feel of worms, their movements, or their home in the soil? After observation of and discussion with the children, the caregiver plans activities to respond to their interests.

Themes for toddlers and two-year-olds are simple and must be related to their experiences in the world. The themes may be from everyday experiences such as eating and dressing, or from a favorite play material such as balls. Or, as seen in the example above, they may be interested in insects and animals, and exposure to a new creature, like the worm, suddenly focuses their interest on a specific type of animal or insect.

The children's interests become themes around which one can organize ideas for activities. Once a theme is suggested, the caregiver plans activities that relate to different areas of the children's development: emotional, social, intellectual, and physical. In this book, we have used the following areas:

- Understanding self (self care and self)
- Understanding others (social relationships with peers)
- Communicating with others (speaking, reading, writing)
- Understanding the world (discovery and creative expression, such as art and music)
- Moving around and making things work.

The Guide to Theme Planning Areas offers a way to plan for these areas by using centers in the classroom. For example, when planning a theme on bread, the creative expression activity might be making playdough, since this material allows a child to create bakery items.

A theme may last for different amounts of time, depending on the children's interests. Some materials might be very attractive to children and they may play with these for a long time. Caregivers might make up a song about the theme and this song might be sung for months at the children's request. Some activities and themes take several weeks to do. For example, a project on bread might take two weeks to complete. In the first week, the children eat different types of bread and talk about its smell, taste, color, and which children eat this type of bread at home. In the second week, you might bake some bread in the classroom, and in the third week, visit a bakery.

Some themes suggest activities in some of the planning areas but not all of them. Try to include one activity in at least two of the centers every day. Toddlers and two-year-olds play for short time periods, so they will appreciate more than one choice. Make sure that planning over the year is varied and includes activities in all the centers.

One note of caution is necessary with theme planning. Try to find a balance of theme planning and child-initiated play. Most day-to-day learning of toddlers and two-year-olds involves practicing with favorite materials. Children love repetition and return often to the same toys and materials. When planning for themes, try to include their familiar activities. You might add new materials and keep some of the favorites as well. For example, making playdough is suggested for the bread theme. Some children enjoy making and playing with playdough and will benefit from connecting this with making bread. For children who do not choose to make playdough and want to play with other creative materials, make sure there are other choices, for example, the easel and paints.

One way to reach a balance of planning themes and child-initiated play is to introduce one theme a month. It is not necessary to have a theme for every month of the year. The children might continue with their individual interests most of the month and focus on a group interest for only a part of the month. If an activity for the theme is interesting to them, continue this for longer than one week. In this way, the caregiver offers connected experiences that do not dominate the individual child's play.

Planning for Mixed Age Groups

Toddlers and two-year-olds may be mixed in the same group. In some classrooms, infants might also be present. Try to plan activities that include a range of ages. For example, when choosing songs around a theme, think of two: a simple song for the younger children and a more complex song for the two-year-olds. This allows the younger child to participate in the theme at his own level. Some activities will be interesting to the older child but not the younger child. If the activity on a table is printing, include simple printing items for toddlers and enough play materials in other parts of the room for the mobile infants.

Sample Themes

Five themes are outlined in the following pages: Bread, Balls, Farm Animals, Pockets, and Water. The activities that are marked with an asterisk (*) are included in this chapter. Some activities from each theme are included in previous chapters and the location of these is indicated in parentheses.

GUIDE FOR PLANNING A THEME

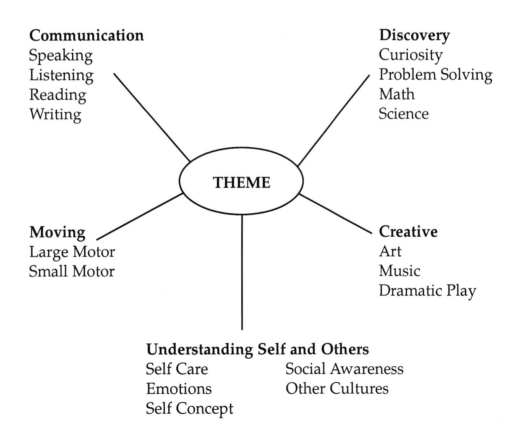

Communication
Speaking
Listening
Reading
Writing

Discovery
Curiosity
Problem Solving
Math
Science

THEME

Moving
Large Motor
Small Motor

Creative
Art
Music
Dramatic Play

Understanding Self and Others
Self Care   Social Awareness
Emotions   Other Cultures
Self Concept

SAMPLE THEME—BREAD

Communication

Talk about bread for meals
Listen to story, *Bread*
Flannel board story The Gingerbread Man

Discovery

Make bread
Compare dry and wet ingredients
Observe bread rising

Moving

Practice kneading playdough (Chapter 5)
Bread making tools in sensory table

Creative

Make playdough (Chapter 5)
Fill empty bread bags with
    crumpled paper to make loaves
Song about bread
Bread-making tools in dramatic
    center

 **Understanding Self and Others**

Spread margarine or jam on bread
Talk about what type of bread families eat
Have parents visit and make bread
Make playdough or loaves for each other

Field Trip: Go to a bakery or other place where bread is sold.

SAMPLE THEME—BALLS

Communication

Discussion of big balls, small balls
Make a book about balls

Discovery

Washing balls in the sensory table
Balls and Tubes*

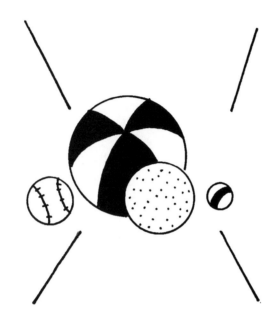

Moving

Place different balls in sensory table
Move ping pong balls with tongs
Ball Game*
Throwing Balls (Chapter 3)

Creative

Printing with balls
Ball Songs*
Movement: roll like a ball

Understanding Self and Others

Catching bubbles
Roll the ball to each other (Chapter 3)

* Activities are included on the following pages.

Balls and Tubes

Purpose: The child drops balls through tubes and experiments with sizes and making objects disappear and reappear. The child learns the concepts of large and small. Experiences with objects disappearing and reappearing help the toddler and two-year-old understand object permanence.

Materials: small balls such as golf balls and ping pong balls
paper tubes from paper towels, toilet paper rolls, and packing tubes
plastic tubes
dish tub, box, or sensory table to catch the balls

Preparation:
1. Cut the tubes into different lengths.
2. Place the tubes and balls in a box or dish tub.
3. Plan on 2 to 3 children per box, and up to 6 children at the sensory table. This activity is good for free choice time.

Activity: Observe the children exploring the materials. Show them how to drop a ball through the tube. When the ball is too big, encourage the child to find another ball that is the right size. The children will also come up with more ideas on how to use the tubes and balls.

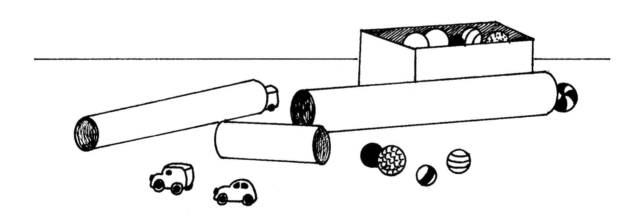

Extensions and Variations:

- Younger toddlers will explore the tubes and balls separately.
- Older children will enjoy using the 2 materials together. Some will be fascinated by longer tubes. See if you can find some clear plastic tubing or pipes for them to experiment with.
- Try using small cars in the tubes.

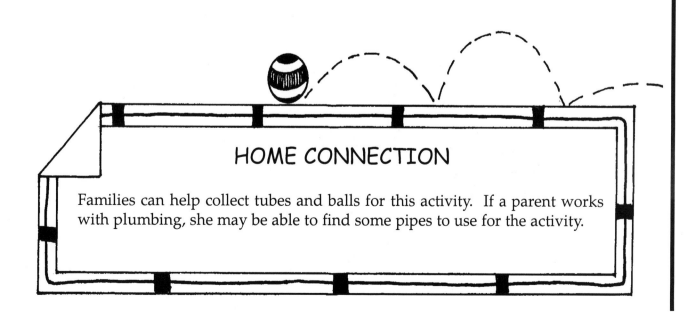

HOME CONNECTION

Families can help collect tubes and balls for this activity. If a parent works with plumbing, she may be able to find some pipes to use for the activity.

Ball Game

Purpose: The child hits a ball that is hanging in the air. This activity challenges the gross motor abilities of the child. The child also practices eye-hand coordination. Playing in pairs encourages social awareness.

Materials: beach ball
yarn or rope
strong tape

Preparation:
1. Attach the yarn or rope to the ball with the strong tape. If you have 2 balls, 4 children can play.
2. Hang the balls from the ceiling, from a piece of climbing equipment, or from a tree branch outside. Make the balls different lengths: one at eye-level and the other just within reach of most toddlers.
3. Help the toddlers to hit the balls, one at a time. After they have mastered it, they will be willing to share and do this in pairs.

Activity: Show the children how to hit the ball. Encourage them by saying, "You reached the ball." Be sure to point out that they should hit the ball and not pull on it. Encourage the older children to hit the ball back and forth to each other. You might demonstrate this with a child.

Extensions and Variations:

- Hang a ball low for younger toddlers.
- Older toddlers may kick a low ball. Help them kick safely if there are children of mixed ages present.
- Old pillow cases filled with crumpled paper can be used instead of balls.

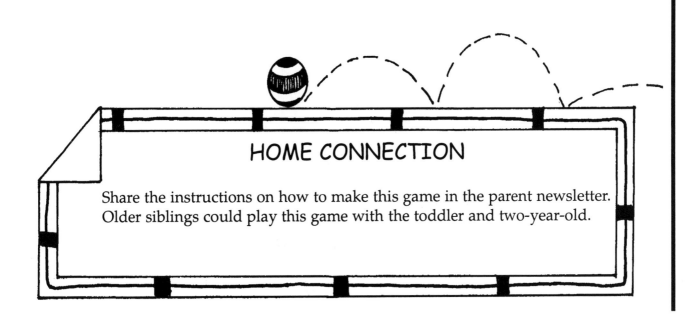

HOME CONNECTION

Share the instructions on how to make this game in the parent newsletter. Older siblings could play this game with the toddler and two-year-old.

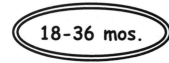

Ball Song About Rolling

Purpose: Children sing the song and examine sizes and colors of balls.

Materials: balls of different sizes

Preparation: Sing this song as children play with balls or group up to 4 in a small circle and sing together.

Activity: Observe children playing with a variety of balls. Sing as they are playing. This song could be sung to a favorite tune, such as "Are You Sleeping?"

Big balls, small balls, big balls, small balls, (show size difference with hands)
See them roll, see them roll. (roll hands)
Round and round in circles, round and round in circles.
Just like this, just like this.

Sing about the color of the balls. As you see children rolling balls, include their names and their actions in the songs.

This song also can be sung without balls, using just the motions.

242

Extensions and Variations:

- Younger children may just explore the ball while you sing. Some may let go of the ball and simply imitate your hand movements.
- Older children will move the ball in the motions of the song.
- Older children can help you sort the balls by size and color into groups.

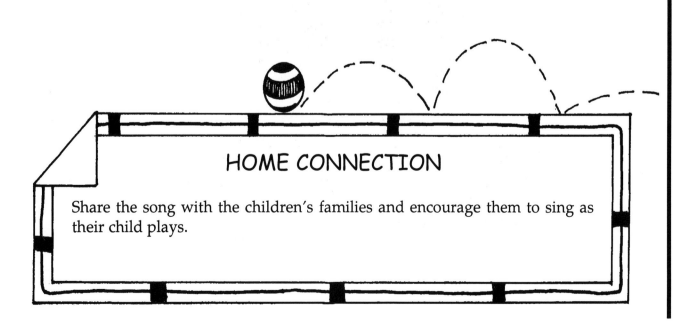

HOME CONNECTION

Share the song with the children's families and encourage them to sing as their child plays.

Ball Song About Throwing

Purpose: Children sing an action song about balls. They practice creative movement and use their large muscles as they move.

Materials: none

Preparation: Use this song with up to 6 children.

Activity: Sing the following to a tune that is familiar to you or the children. For example, this song can be sung to the tune of "Here We Go 'Round the Mulberry Bush." Use large movements as though you are using a very large, imaginary ball.

This is the way we throw the ball, (pretend to throw the ball)
throw the ball, throw the ball.
This is the way we throw the ball
when we play with our friends.

This is the way we catch the ball, (pretend to catch the ball)
catch the ball, catch the ball.
This is the way we catch the ball
when we play with our friends.

Add more verses depending upon the children's interest. You could include kicking the ball, rolling the ball, and for older children, bouncing the ball.

Extensions and Variations:

- Sing this song as you roll the ball to the younger toddler.
- Use real balls with older children inside or outside.

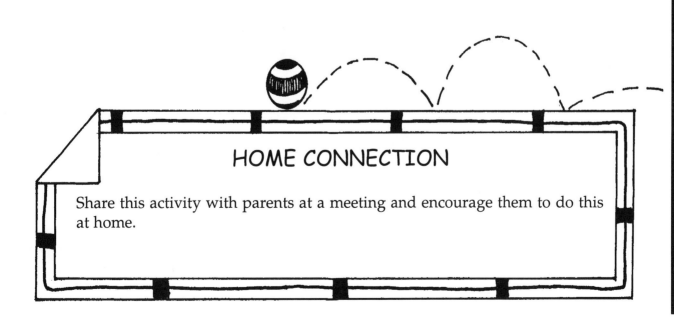

HOME CONNECTION

Share this activity with parents at a meeting and encourage them to do this at home.

FARM ANIMALS

Communication

Stick Puppets*
Flannel board and farm animals

Discovery

Finding Animals*
Match Animal Parents and
Babies*

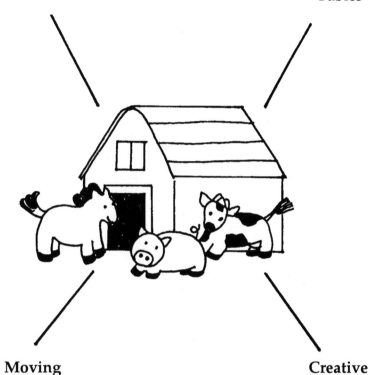

Moving

Wash farm animals in sensory tub
Pretend to move like farm animals

Creative

Animal prints in playdough
Add animals to block area
Song about farm animals

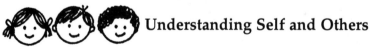 **Understanding Self and Others**

Making Our Farms*

Field Trip Suggestion: A visit to see animals or a farm

* Activities are included on following pages

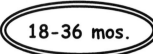

Animal Stick Puppets

Purpose: Children mimic the sounds of an animal as they hold the stick puppet. Songs help the children connect the name of the animal and its sound.

Materials: pictures of farm animals
sticks (such as those used for ice cream)
clear plastic paper to cover the pictures
glue or tape

Preparation:
1. Find pictures of animals in old magazines or draw them.
2. Cut out the pictures and cover them with the plastic.
3. Glue the pictures on the sticks. Make enough for each child to hold one.
4. You can do this activity with an individual child during play time or a small group of up to 6 children.

Activity: Sing or make up a song about the animals. Let the child show you the animals she wants you to sing about. Use a stick puppet and show the children how to move the puppet while singing the song. Move the puppet to the rhythm of the song. Encourage the children to stand up while they sing.

One example of a song with farm animals is "Old MacDonald Had a Farm." Each verse can include a different farm animal:

Old Macdonald had a farm
e i e i o
And on this farm he had a cow
e i e i o
With a moo moo here and a moo moo there
Here a moo, there a moo, everywhere a moo moo.

You can substitute the child's name for the farmer's in this song.

Extensions and Variations:

• Use stuffed animals or plastic animals with younger children.
• Use felt shapes with older children. They can place their shape on the felt board during the song. Leave the felt shapes and board out for the children to play with later.

HOME CONNECTION

Parents can collect used sticks for making the puppets. Display the finished puppets for the family to see.

Finding the Animals

Purpose: Children search for animals in straw or a similar material and practice identifying animals. Animals that disappear and reappear help younger children understand object permanence. Picking up the animals offers practice with small-motor skills.

Materials: variety of small plastic animals
straw or materials to hide the animals in (paper could be used)
box or the sensory table
small box or basket for the animals

Preparation:
1. Fill the table or box with straw or similar material.
2. Place the animals in a small basket or box.
3. This a good activity for choosing time.
4. Two children per box or up to 6 at the sensory table could play together.

Activity: Bring the box of animals to the sensory tub or small box. Suggest to the children that they play a game of hiding. Let each child choose an animal to hide. When the animals are all hidden, encourage the children to find them. Put the box in the middle of the table and tell them it is the barn. They can put the found animals back in it.

As they search, ask them, "What do you feel? Is it an animal? What does the straw feel like?" As the children find the animals, encourage them to make the animal's sound and then put it back into the barn. Keep looking and making animal sounds. The children will probably want to repeat this once the animals have been found.

Extensions and Variations:

- Younger children will enjoy only a few animals. Choose large animals for them.
- Older children may want to use smaller animals. Include a mixture if there are mixed ages and suggest that the older children find only the small animals.

HOME CONNECTION

Find out which play animals the child has at home. Try to have these familiar animals in the activity.

Matching Animals

Purpose: The child matches pictures of adult and baby animals. He learns to sort the animals into groups and also learns the names of animal babies and their parents.

Materials: pictures of animal parents and babies
clear plastic paper
small box or basket

Preparation:
1. Cut out pictures of animal parents and babies.
2. Cover the pictures with clear plastic paper.
3. Put the pictures in a small box or basket.
4. This activity can be placed with other manipulatives and played on a table or rug.
5. Up to 3 children could play together.

Activity: Observe the child exploring the materials. You might point out a baby animal and its parents. "Josef, here is a baby cow. It is called a calf. Which animal is the mother? What is she called?" Place these pictures together and ask the child if he knows the sound they make. Encourage the child to choose another animal and to put the baby animal with its parents. Continue for as long as the child is interested.

Extensions and Variations:

- Younger toddlers will explore and name the animals, but will not distinguish adults and babies.
- Older children will be able to sort the animals into family groups.

HOME CONNECTION

Ask the parents if the child has seen animal parents and babies. Include these animals in the pictures.

Making Our Farms

Purpose: The child uses blocks, paper, and animals to make a farm for imaginary play. Children can cooperate to make one farm or make neighboring farms.

Materials: wooden, plastic, or stuffed farm animals
small blocks or sticks for fences
yellow paper for bales of hay
orange paper for carrots
red paper for apples
masking tape

Preparation:
1. Gather a variety of farm animals.
2. Use a corner of the floor or a low table to define the group farm.
3. For neighboring farms, use masking tape to outline the boundaries of each farm.
4. Cut out paper shapes for carrots, apples, and hay.
5. Place the blocks nearby for the children to build fences, sheds, and other things.
6. Depending on the amount of materials and ability of the children to work together, up to 4 children might be able to play with a group farm at a time.

Activity: Tell the children that they can make farms. Provide blocks to build barns or sheds. If necessary, you could show the children how to build one. Encourage the children to feed the animals hay, apples, or carrots. They may think of other foods for the animals. They can cut out shapes for food or ask you to make some more. While playing on the farm, talk with the children about the names of the animals, how to care for the animals, and how to help their neighbors with their animals. Add books for the children to look at as they build the farm.

Extensions and Variations:

• Younger children will prefer to play with the animals. If the older children want to have lots of small items in their farms, put the farms on a table away from the younger toddlers.

• Older children can learn about individual work space when the tape is used to designate separate farms. The tape is a visual reminder of their work space.

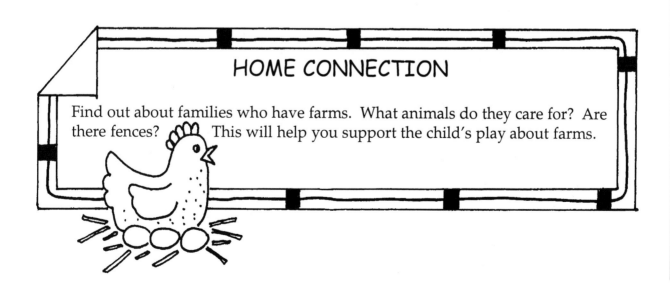

HOME CONNECTION

Find out about families who have farms. What animals do they care for? Are there fences? This will help you support the child's play about farms.

SAMPLE THEME—POCKETS

Communicating

Discussion of individual pockets
Book: *A Pocket for Corduroy*

Discovery

What Is in My Pocket?*
Matching Pockets*

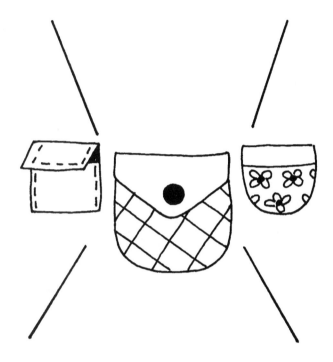

Moving

Pocket Dance*
Put small objects in pocket
dramatic play center

Creative

Song about pockets
Clothes with pockets in them

Understanding Self and Others

Pocket Day—A discussion of everyone's pockets
Act the story of animals living in a pocket

* Activities are included on the following pages.

Matching Pockets

Purpose: Children match fabric pockets on a teacher-made pocket game. The activity encourages using visual discrimination skills to match patterns. Children practice their small-motor skills as they place the fabric in the pocket.

Materials: fabric or paper of 3 or 4 different patterns
large piece of thick paper or cardboard for the background
small piece of thick paper or cardboard for the backs of the rectangles
glue
scissors
clear plastic for covering the pockets
utility blade
envelope

Preparation: 1. Cut pocket shapes from the fabric or paper.
2. Glue the "pockets" on the large piece of paper. Leave the top seam open.
3. Cut rectangles or "handkerchiefs" out of the same material to fit in the pockets.
4. Glue the rectangles to thick paper to make them easy to handle.
5. Cover the pockets with clear plastic. After gluing, open the top seam of the pocket with the utility blade or scissors.
6. Use the envelope to store the rectangles. Attach the envelope to the back of the large piece of paper.
7. This game is good for 2 children at a time. Place the game with other matching and sorting play materials and let children choose it.

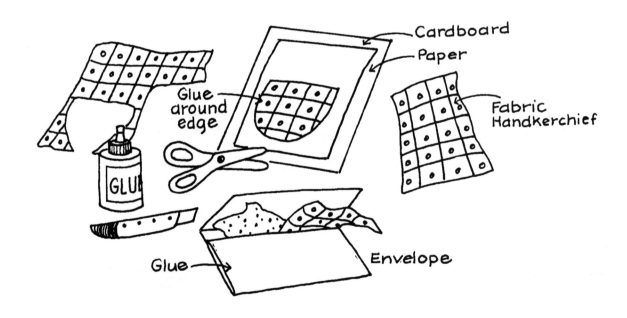

Cardboard
Paper
Glue around edge
Fabric Handkerchief
GLUE
Glue
Envelope

Activity: Observe the children exploring the game. Encourage them to match the handkerchief and the pockets. "Julia, can you find the same pattern for this handkerchief?" Some children will find it a challenge to match 1 or 2 patterns at first. If the child is having difficulty, cover up all but 2 pockets and this will make it easier. Children may want to repeat this once they have matched the pockets. Encourage them to do so.

Extensions and Variations:

• Younger toddlers will enjoy putting handkerchiefs in pockets without matching them.
• Children who have difficulty seeing will benefit from enlarged pockets made of fabric with simple patterns. Two pockets are enough to start with.

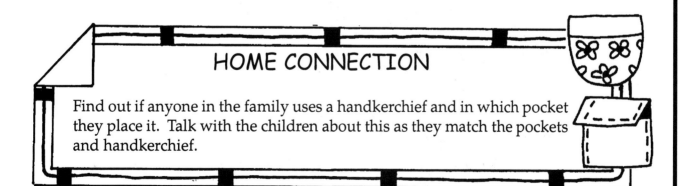

HOME CONNECTION

Find out if anyone in the family uses a handkerchief and in which pocket they place it. Talk with the children about this as they match the pockets and handkerchief.

What Is in My Pocket?

Purpose: The child hides and discovers objects in pockets. They must figure out what size object fits in the pocket. This activity encourages language use as the child speaks about what is in the pocket. Putting objects in and taking them out of pockets provides good practice with small-motor skills.

Materials: aprons
small objects that fit in a pocket

Preparation:
1. Make sure everyone wears clothing with pockets for the day, including the caregivers. Those without pockets can use an apron.
2. The caregiver can begin the activity by placing a small object in her pocket.
3. Do this activity during choice time as children are playing. Up to 3 children at a time can play this. This allows everyone to speak about their object.
4. This activity also can be done outside, since most jackets have pockets.

Activity: The caregiver might begin with a simple poem.

(Caregiver name), (Caregiver name), our teacher
Had a tiny bear and couldn't keep her.
She put her in her pocket for sure
And there she kept her quite secure!

Ask the child to bring you an object from the room or outside to put in your pocket. Change the poem to include the new item. The child might like to put an object in her pocket. She might try first with the object you used. Then find one for her, put it in her pocket, and sing the song together. If other children have joined you, give each child a chance to find an object and to have an object in her pocket.

After each child has had a turn, ask the children to find objects for each other. They will need your help chanting the poem. Some will delight in finding objects and placing them in their own pockets and then showing them to other children.

Extensions and Variations:

• Younger children will enjoy taking things in and out of their own pockets and yours.
• Older children might enjoy having a small basket of objects to choose from. Collect these ahead of time and make sure they are large enough to avoid choking hazards.

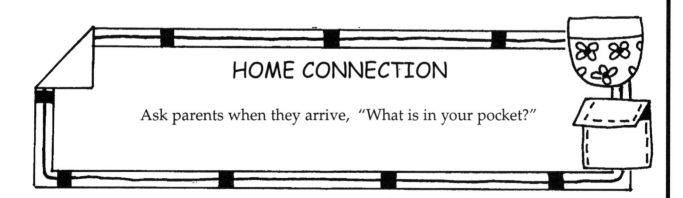

HOME CONNECTION

Ask parents when they arrive, "What is in your pocket?"

Pocket Dance

Purpose: Children dance with their hands in their pockets. They practice moving with their upper body and legs. Their ability to balance is challenged by this dance.

Materials: none

Preparation:
1. Choose a song for dancing. You might use an instrument to create a dance rhythm.
2. A small group of 4 to 8 children can dance at one time. Do this during choice time or music time.

Activity: Begin by singing or playing the dance music. Put your hands in your pockets and ask the children to do this as well. If some do not have pockets, they can put their hands on their hips, or use aprons with pockets. Give simple directions such as, "Remember, put your hands in your pocket and dance." Encourage them to dance. Demonstrate by moving your upper body from side to side, moving your head up and down, shaking a leg at a time, jumping up and down, and tapping your toes. Some children will automatically remove their hands from their pockets to clap. Be accepting of this. Encourage them to keep their hands in their pockets, but remember it is difficult for children to do this for a long time while dancing.

Extensions and Variations:

• The younger child will dance and sway to the music. He might put his hand in his pocket.
• Children who have difficulty balancing will do better with their hands out of their pockets. They can put their hands in their pockets before dancing and then at the end.

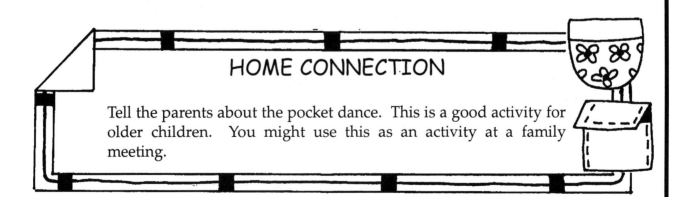

HOME CONNECTION

Tell the parents about the pocket dance. This is a good activity for older children. You might use this as an activity at a family meeting.

SAMPLE THEME—WATER

Communication

Read books about baths
Listen to water sounds
Making Bubbles*
Observe water outside

Discovery

Put warm and cold water in tubs
Making Rain*

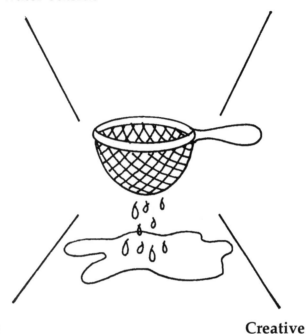

Moving

Squirt bottles outside
Washing chairs (Chapter 5)
Make raindrops with eyedroppers (Chapter 5)
Puddle Jumps*

Creative

Water Painting*
Songs about rain

 **Understanding Self and Others**

Catching bubbles
Washing Up (Chapter 5)

Field Trip Suggestion: Take a walk in the rain.

*Activities are included on the following pages.

Making Rain

Purpose: Children make rain using sieves and strainers in water. They can observe the shape and sound of rain, and the process of rain falling. Playing with rain is satisfying and helps a child feel confident.

Materials: dish tub or sensory table
strainers
strainer toys made from empty plastic food containers and empty cans
empty food containers with no holes
waterproof smocks

Preparation: 1. Make strainers by poking holes in the plastic food containers or empty cans.
2. Place water in the dish tub or sensory table. The water should be deep enough to fill the strainers half way, but not too deep as children will spill it.
3. Place a variety of strainers, strainer toys, and empty containers in the sensory table.
4. Plan on 2 children to a dish tub or up to 6 in the sensory table.

Activity: Tell the children they can make rain with these toys. Help them put on smocks. Encourage them to fill the strainers with water and hold them high. The "rain" will fall out of the strainer into the sensory table. As they play, describe their actions. "Alexander, you made the water go drip, drip. Does it sound like rain?" "Alexander is making a lot of rain and it is falling very quickly." Children love to play with water and will stay at this activity for quite a while.

Extensions and Variations:

- Younger children will use the strainers to move the water and splash. They might practice with the concept of water falling down from the strainer. Encourage them to let the water fall into the tub, and not on the floor.
- Go for a walk in the rain and talk with the older children about how rain falls. Sing songs about rain as you walk.
- Use strainers to strain flour or salt inside. Use strainers for dirt outside.

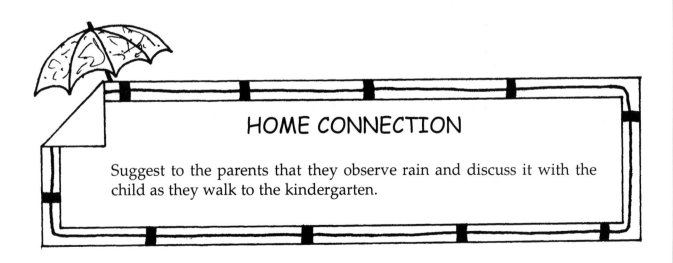

HOME CONNECTION

Suggest to the parents that they observe rain and discuss it with the child as they walk to the kindergarten.

Making Bubbles

Purpose: Children use a variety of tools with water to make bubbles. They learn about what actions make bubbles and properties of bubbles.

Materials:
dish tubs or sensory table
liquid dish soap
basters
wire whisks
empty or almost empty dish soap bottles
smocks

Preparation:
1. Put water in the dish tubs and sensory table, approximately 3" or 8 cm. deep.
2. Add a small amount of dish soap. Stir the soap and water to make sure bubbles form.
3. Collect the basters, wire whisks, and dish soap bottles and put them in the tubs.
4. This is a good activity during choice time. Up to 2 children per dish tub or 6 at the sensory table could play at one time.

Activity: Tell the children that they can make bubbles with the tools. Help them put on smocks before they begin. Show the children how to squeeze the basters in the water and make bubbles. Show them how to squeeze the bottles in the water and watch the bubbles come out. You can ask them about the bubbles. "Are they big? Small? Where did the bubbles come from?" Show the children how to whip the water with the whisks. Ask, "What happens to the water?" Describe what individual children are doing as they experiment. Be sure to point out the sounds the air makes as they squeeze the baster and bottles.

Extensions and Variations:

* Younger children will make bubbles by swirling the water with their hands or large spoons. They will enjoy touching the bubbles and making them move.
* Give the older children spoons and encourage them to catch the bubbles.
* Use this recipe and add a teaspoon of glycerine to blow bubbles outside. The glycerine makes the bubbles last longer. You can make bubble blowers with small pieces of wire or cut large holes in the lids of empty food containers.

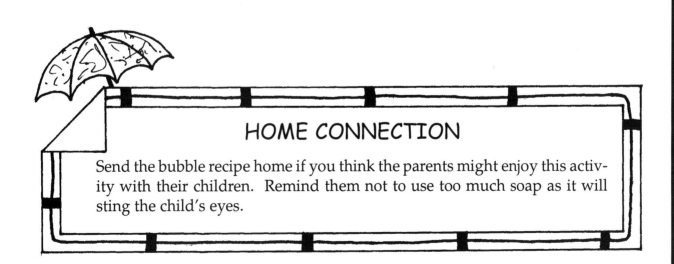

HOME CONNECTION

Send the bubble recipe home if you think the parents might enjoy this activity with their children. Remind them not to use too much soap as it will sting the child's eyes.

Water Painting

Purpose: Children "paint" with water. They make patterns and practice brush strokes. They use their imaginations as they pretend to be real painters. As the water dries, they observe properties of wet and dry.

Materials: house painting brushes
cans or plastic milk bottles
string

Preparation:
1. Poke holes in the cans and attach string to the cans. The strings should be long enough to hang around a child's neck.
2. Cut holes in the plastic milk bottles so the bottle becomes a bucket with a handle.
3. This is an individual activity, so have a brush for each child The activity can be done inside or outside.

Activity: Fill a can or bucket half-full and place a brush nearby. When children come over to see what you are doing, tell them they can paint with water. Give each child a bucket and brush. Suggest they use the brush to paint the furniture. If you are outside, they can paint the wall or playground equipment. Describe their work as they paint. "Anna, you are painting the shelf a dark color. You are using big strokes with your brush." As the water dries, ask the children why the painted object is changing colors.

The children will be fascinated and some will want to continue painting for a long time. Make sure you have enough brushes and cans for the children who are waiting to paint.

Extensions and Variations:

- Younger children will need brushes with large handles and cans with wide openings. They will enjoy the sensory experience. Water feels cool on their skin.
- Older children might enjoy making painter's hats to wear while they paint.
- A visit to observe painters would add to this activity.

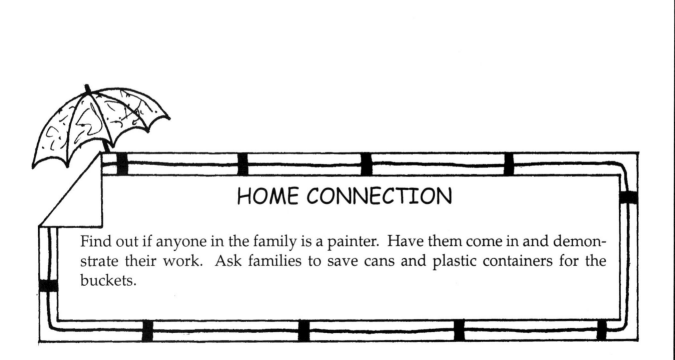

HOME CONNECTION

Find out if anyone in the family is a painter. Have them come in and demonstrate their work. Ask families to save cans and plastic containers for the buckets.

Puddle Jumps

Purpose: Children pretend to jump over puddles and practice their jumping skills. They enjoy moving their bodies and can better understand the concept of "over" as they jump.

Materials: blue paper
scissors
tape

Preparation:
1. Make sure you have a large open area inside or outside.
2. Cut 4 to 6 puddles out of the paper.
3. If you are playing inside, arrange the puddles about 8 to 12 inches (20-30 cm.) apart and tape them to the floor. If you are outside, lay the puddles on the ground.
4. This game works well for individuals and groups of 4 to 6 children.

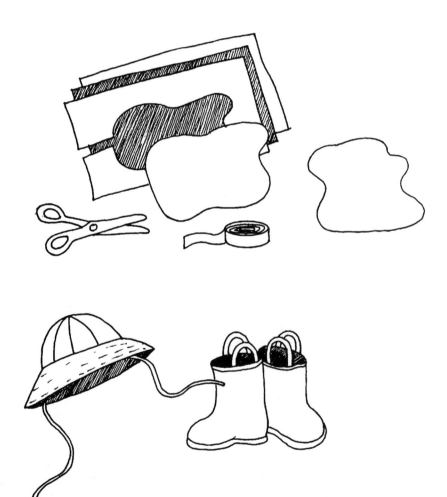

Activity: As children come over, explain the game to them. "Peter, these are pretend puddles. Show me if you can jump over one." You might demonstrate. The child can then follow you. Describe how the child jumps: "Peter, you jumped over the puddle. You jumped with both feet." Provide lots of encouragement. "What a big jump!" "You jumped high that time." Invite other children to join in as they come over. Comment on how 2 children are jumping together.

Extensions and Variations:

- Younger children might like to step over the puddles.
- Vary the shapes of the puddles. You could use geometric shapes.
- Vary the colors of the puddles.
- Add rain hats or boots while jumping the puddles.
- Take a walk in the rain and jump real puddles.

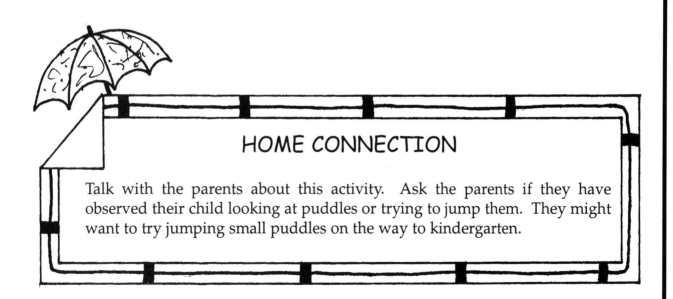

HOME CONNECTION

Talk with the parents about this activity. Ask the parents if they have observed their child looking at puddles or trying to jump them. They might want to try jumping small puddles on the way to kindergarten.

Chapter Seven:

Families and Communities

Involving Families and Communities

Families

The most important people in the lives of infants and toddlers are the adults who care for them, their parents first and foremost. The entire family, siblings, aunts, uncles, cousins, and grandparents, have a special role for young children. Families are sources of love, identity, and security. They also provide a lot of new information and learning.

Activities that help infants and toddlers learn about their families and about families of other children are an important part of each child's development. This chapter offers caregivers activity ideas that relate to family roles, family members, family traditions, and family celebrations. These learning activities give young children the opportunity to play out aspects of family life, for example, taking care of babies and visiting relatives. Through their play, children develop a better sense of what it means to be in a family. The activities also connect each young child emotionally to his family, which provides additional support while the child is separate from the family during the day.

Communities

Along with families, the community is a source of support and learning. Infants and toddlers learn everyday about people and places in their community as they accompany their caregivers to the park, to the store, and to the child care program. This chapter includes activities to help infants and toddlers explore their surroundings, including places in the neighborhood and working in the community. Young children are interested in work clothes and tools. By pretending to be a baker, they learn about the baker's job and about bread.

Who Is on the Picture Cube?

Purpose: The child identifies members of her family. The adult makes the picture cube and plays a guessing game with the child. This game is important for the child's growing sense of self and family. The child over 2 can help glue the pictures on the cube, using her small muscles and her creativity. The older child practices speaking names and talking about family members.

Materials: old picture of each child's family that the family will let you cut up
picture of each child that you take in the classroom
paper cartons such as milk cartons or juice cartons
glue
markers
plastic paper to protect the pictures

Preparation:
1. Make the cube by cutting the carton in half. Flatten the top peak of the carton by folding over the peak and gluing or taping the edge. (See illustration.) Fit the top half into the bottom to make a cube. Tape the edges of the 2 pieces of carton.
2. Cut individual family members (mother, father, brother, sister) from the photo and glue one person on each side of the cube. Glue a picture of the child on one side.
3. Cover the photos with plastic paper so they will last longer.
4. This activity can be done with up to 3 children at a time.

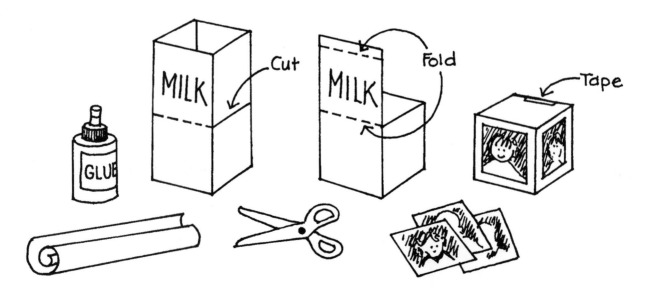

Activity: Sit on the floor with a child or a small group of children. Play the guessing game with one child at a time. Ask the child, "Whose picture is this?" If you have a group of children, be sure that each child gets a turn.

If you have a group of mixed ages, let the younger children explore the cube.

Ask the children over 2 years of age to tell you who is on the cube, and encourage them to name people on other sides of the cube.

Extensions and Variations:

• Include pictures of grandparents and other relatives on the cube.
• Make a cube of all the children in the group. This is a good activity for learning names.
• Use large photos for children who have difficulty seeing.

HOME CONNECTION

Make sure family members are willing to let you cut their picture for this activity. If they don't want you to cut it, glue the family picture on one side of the cube and draw objects for the child to identify on the other sides. Send the child's cube home so the family can play the game at home.

Making a Necklace for Mom

Purpose: Children practice fine-motor skills as they string objects to make necklaces for their mothers or other important people in their lives. Children learn the feelings of caring for others by making and giving a gift.

Materials: string (thick string or yarn is easier for younger children)
tape for the ends of the string
stringing objects such as buttons, small pieces of plastic, or paper straws
containers for holding objects

Preparation:
1. Cut pieces of string for the necklaces.
2. Tie a knot at one end of the string. Place tape on the other end of the string to make stringing easier.
3. Place objects for stringing in 2 containers on a low table or the floor.
4. This activity can include a small group of up to 6 children with an adult. It is important for sufficient numbers of adults to be present to ensure that the younger children do not swallow the stringing objects.

Activity: Invite the child to make a necklace for her mother or another family member. Fathers like anything made by their child and this includes necklaces too. Give each child a string and point to the stringing objects. "Julia, you can put these pretty buttons on the string to make a necklace." Make a sample with a few pieces to show the process of stringing. Younger children will need help stringing the beads. Hold the string and let them place the object on it. Two-year-olds will need help with the first object and then they will want to hold the string and string objects independently. Give them lots of encouragement to keep going.

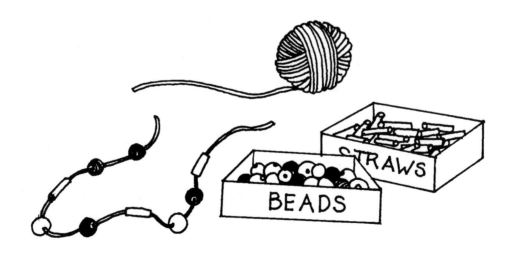

Each child will work for a different amount of time and will make a unique necklace. A child might string just one bead, another might use many beads. When the child indicates she is finished, tie the ends of her necklace together, write her name on it, and put it in a special place so the child will remember to take it home. Some children will want to wear their creations before putting them away.

Extensions and Variations:

- Wooden beads can be used to make necklaces and these can be kept in the classroom instead of sending them home. Keep a shoe box full of beads and string for this activity.
- Younger children will enjoy touching and looking at colored wooden bead necklaces.
- Older children can make necklaces with small playdough pieces. The children and the caregiver can make the playdough together and then form small pieces with it. The adult makes a small hole in each of the pieces and dries them on a tray before the children string them.

HOME CONNECTION

This activity can also be done at a parent meeting to show parents how to use simple household objects to make crafts. The parent and child could make a necklace for grandmother.

Taking Care of Baby

Purpose: The child plays with different dolls and practices caring for them. This play helps the child understand how parents care for babies. The child also learns to identify the emotions of caring for others.

Materials: different dolls (different races and with assorted colors and types of hair)
scarves
doll clothes
boxes or baskets for scarves and doll clothes

Preparation: 1. Place the dolls, scarves, and clothes on a rug or in the dramatic play area.
2. Use separate containers for the clothes and the scarves.
3. This activity can be done with a child or a small group of up to 4 children.

Activity: Invite the children to take care of the dolls. "Peter, would you like to carry the baby? You could be the father and carry the baby." Encourage the child who is not yet walking to explore the baby. "Marina, feel the baby's hair. Is it curly? Where is your hair? " The children can carry the dolls in their arms or in slings made out of a scarves. Encourage them to rock and sing to the babies. Ask the children if the babies are tired or hungry. Each child might want to care for the baby in a different way. One might want to carry the baby, another to rock it to sleep. As you help the child care for the baby in different ways, the child learns about the various tasks adults perform when caring for babies.

Extensions and Variations:

- The younger child is learning body parts. Help identify the hair, eyes, nose, mouth, and other parts.
- Older children like to dress the baby. They can use the scarves for blankets as well. They may need the adult to demonstrate how to dress and feed the baby.

HOME CONNECTION

Find out how each family carries and rocks the baby. There are differences in how families care for babies. Consider asking parents for a picture of them feeding or holding their child and make a picture book of all the families taking care of children.

Homes

Purpose: Children use their imagination to build a house for the whole group. They learn about homes by building and playing in one. The children use their small muscles to build the house and their large muscles as they crawl in and out of it.

Materials: big boxes, chairs, or a table
sheets or light materials to cover the house
tape to secure the cloth edges

Preparation: 1. Clear a section of the room to be used for the house.
2. Toddlers and two-year-olds will enjoy helping construct the house.
3. Start with a simple house. It could be under a table or a sheet draped over 2 pieces of furniture.
4. Build the house with a small group of up to 3 children and then let up to 4 play at one time.

Activity: Children will notice this activity right away and come over to investigate. Explain that you are building a home to play in. Encourage 3 children to be builders and the rest to be the family who will live there. Make sure there are interesting choices in the rest of the classroom in case too many children want to help build. The builders can help put on the roof and tape it to the furniture. They will want to crawl inside immediately. Make sure there is enough space in the home for up to 6 children.

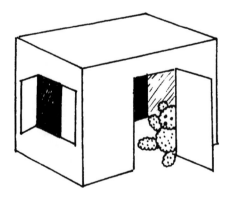

Talk with the children about different types of homes: apartments, huts, tents, cabins, caves, to name a few. The children will want to play with this home for more than one activity period. Interest may last for weeks.

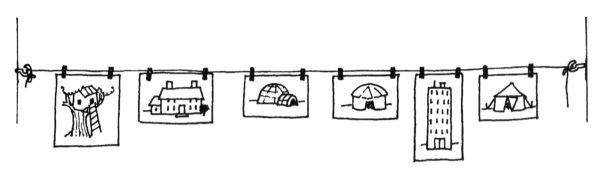

Extensions and Variations:

- Collect pictures of different types of homes and display these so children can look at them and discuss them. Cover the pictures with plastic and place them at the children's eye-level.
- Place some of these pictures in the dramatic play area and encourage the children to talk about their homes as they play.
- Cut pictures of different homes from magazines. Make a group collage of different homes by pasting the pictures on a large sheet of paper.

HOME CONNECTION

Ask each family to draw or take a photograph of the child's home. Make a display of the homes for the children to look at. Put the display in a notebook or on the wall.

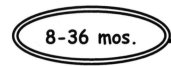

Sounds Around Grandfather's Home

Purpose: The child listens to and identifies the sounds of grandfather's home.

Materials: audiocassette recorder
blank audiocassette

Preparation:
1. Ask parents what sounds the children might hear in their grandfather's home. These might be sounds that are also in the child's home, such as doors slamming, dogs barking, water coming out of a faucet, or a radio playing. Find out if there is a sound that is specific to the grandparents' home.
2. Make a list of sounds that all the children might find in their own home or in their grandfather's home. Try for 5 to 7 sounds. Record the sound long enough for the child to be able to identify it easily.
3. Sit on the floor with the children and the recorder and tape.
4. This activity works best with up to 3 children.

Activity: Encourage the children to listen to the sounds. "Peter, would you like to hear the sounds of grandfather's home?" Play a sound and observe the child. Ask, "What's that? Is it a dog?" You might identify the sounds at first if the child does not know what to call them. Repeat the sounds so the child will identify themmore easily. It will take time for the child to become familiar with the tape recorder and the sounds.

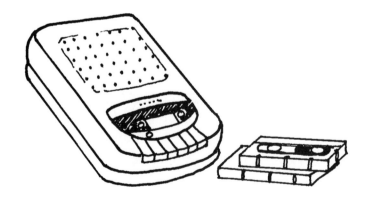

Extensions and Variations:

• The younger children will listen to the sounds but not identify them. They will be fascinated by the recorder and want to touch it.
• Older children might be interested in exploring the sounds of the classroom. You could tape some sounds and use them in the game.
• Take a walk outside and listen to the neighborhood sounds.

HOME CONNECTION

Talk with the parents about sounds in the child's home and the grandparents' home. Make sure you have some similar sounds on the tape. The parents can listen for sounds at home with their child. Find out if the grandparents live with the child. If they do, sounds from the child's home will work well. If they don't, include a sound similar to one found in the grandparent's home.

Grandmother's Tale

Purpose: The adult tells a favorite story of the child's grandmother to the child and a small group. The story provides a language experience and the child learns new words. The child also learns about his grandmother and the family's culture from the story.

Preparation:
1. Ask the parents for the tales or stories their grandparents told them when they were small. Ask the parent to come tell the story. If the parent is unable to do so, write the story down and tell it yourself.
2. This story can be told to an individual or a small group of up to 4 children.

Activity: Find a comfortable place to sit on the floor or in a rocking chair. Introduce the tale by explaining that grandparents have stories they tell their children. When these children grow up and are parents, they tell their children the same story. Tell the children which child's parents or grandparents tell this story. "This is a story that Josef's grandmother tells his mother and him." Children will often say "Again!" and want you to tell the story a second time. They love stories associated with grandparents.

Extensions and Variations:

• Some old tales are also found in children's books. If possible, find a book with a traditional tale, and read it to the children. Leave the book in the book area for the children to explore.
• Younger children like sitting in your lap and listening to your voice.
• Older children like to discuss their grandparents after hearing a story. This is a wonderful chance for them to practice speaking and to learn about family from different regions.
• Invite a storyteller to come and tell the traditional or grandparent tales.

HOME CONNECTION

Having a family member come to tell this story is the best way to do this activity. If they are busy or live far away, the next best thing is for you to tell it.

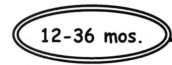

Visit by a Family Musician

Purpose: A family member comes and sings a favorite song. Children listen and sing along. The activity offers children a language experience and they learn more about family members.

Preparation: 1. Ask family members if there is someone who will come to sing a favorite song.
2. This activity could include a small group or the whole group of children.

Activity: Find or clear a space for the group to sit or stand. Introduce the activity by telling the children that a child's family member will come to sing a song. The children will enjoy this activity more if they can clap or dance as the musician sings. They could listen once and then learn the song a second time. Some children will stay and listen a long time while others will listen only once and then go off to play.

Extensions and Variations:

- Make a songbook of songs told to you by the children's relatives.
- Sing and make music using simple instruments made out of bells on strings.
- Collect pictures of family members singing and dancing, and display these for the children.

HOME CONNECTION

Ask parents about favorite songs in their family. Lullabies will be especially meaningful for children of this age.

Going Over the Mountain to Visit

Purpose: The child pretends to go on a trip to visit relatives. The visit involves going over the mountain and the child learns the concept of over. This activity improves the infant's coordination and gives her an opportunity to use her large muscles as she practices crawling.

Materials: 4 to 5 soft pillows

Preparation:
1. Collect pillows and make a pile of them to create a mountain for climbing on.
2. Do this activity with 1 or 2 children.

Activity: Sit on the floor near the pillows. Encourage the child to come and climb. As the child climbs the pillows, you might say "Marina, we are climbing up the pillows. Good climbing. You are going up a big mountain to visit Aunt Julia. Climb, climb, climb." Children will enjoy climbing. If the pillows are unsteady and keep moving, take a couple away to simplify the activity.

Extensions and Variations:

- Older toddlers and two-year-olds will like making their own mountain when the pillows fall down.
- Find a book about mountains and show the children the pictures.
- Make up a story about going over the mountain to visit a relative.

HOME CONNECTION

Many families have relatives who live at a distance. Find out who goes over the mountains or up big hills when they travel to visit these relatives. You can include these names as the children play.

Family Fabrics and Clothes

Purpose: Children learn about traditional fabrics and clothing designs as they explore different materials and clothes. Infants and toddlers learn about the clothes by touching and seeing different fabrics. Toddlers and two-year-olds use their imaginations as they wear the clothes and pretend to be other members of the family.

Materials: pieces of fabric for traditional family clothing
old shirts, skirts, or other used traditional clothing
pictures from magazines or of family members wearing clothing with these fabrics

Preparation:
1. Ask the families for ideas on fabrics for traditional clothes. These might be clothes worn everyday or for celebrations.
2. Collect fabrics for traditional clothes and some old clothing.
3. Place the different fabrics in a basket or shoe box for children to explore.
4. This activity may be done with up to 3 children and an adult.

Activity: Choose a place on the rug or low table to place the fabric and clothes. Let the children explore the textures. Ask them questions about the fabric, "Peter, is the cloth soft or scratchy?" Observe the children to see what interests them. Do they like to rub the cloth on their skin, look at it in the light, and wave it to see how it moves? If they are unsure what to do with the cloth, you might suggest some of these actions. After they explore the fabric, mention that shirts and skirts for dancing in are made out of this cloth. If you have large pieces of fabric, the children may want to dance with them.

Extensions and Variations:

- Place the clothes in the dramatic play area for toddlers and two-year-olds. They can dress up and pretend they are family members doing traditional work and celebrating.
- Glue the pieces of fabric on a shoe box or a piece of thick paper for younger children to touch.

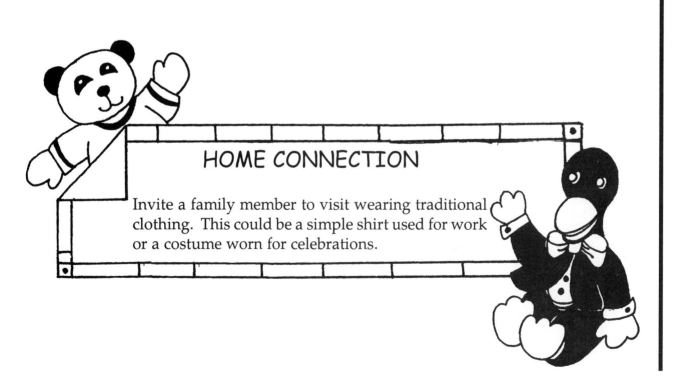

HOME CONNECTION

Invite a family member to visit wearing traditional clothing. This could be a simple shirt used for work or a costume worn for celebrations.

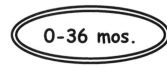

Family Songs and Dances

Purpose: Children sing and dance, and learn about different family celebrations.

Materials: collection of songs and dances from different family celebrations

Preparation:
1. Collect songs and dances from families. You might use audiotapes of the music.
2. Singing and dancing can include a small or large group.

Activity: Find a place large enough for the group. Play or sing a few different songs to introduce the children to the music. Choose a song or dance with simple words and movements for the children to learn. Some groups of children may not have lots of diversity in celebrations. In this case, consider offering a song and dance that is different from their family celebrations.

Extensions and Variations:

- Invite a family member to teach the children the song or dance. Older siblings might know the songs and be willing to come and teach them to the infants and toddlers.
- Use simple instruments to accompany the music. Each child can shake a bell or beat on a simple drum while the visitor sings or dances.

HOME CONNECTION

Ask family members about the regions they come from and traditional songs and dances of that region. They might know of a musician who can visit and perform for the children.

Celebration Cards

Purpose: Children make cards to send to family members. They practice writing and develop small muscle skills. Sending cards is exciting and children enjoy feelings of giving to other family members.

Materials: old greeting cards for celebrations (births, weddings, Christmas, Hanukkah)
envelopes and old stationery
markers or crayons
basket or box for cards

Preparation: 1. Collect different types of cards, old stationery, and envelopes.
2. Place the cards in a basket or box for children to look at.
3. Include up to 4 children in this activity.

Activity: Place the cards, markers, stationery, and envelopes on a small table. Encourage the children to look at the cards and talk about the different celebrations the cards are used for. Let the children use the markers to decorate the cards. They might tell you what to write on the cards. The older children might use envelopes. Ask the children if they would like to send the card to a parent, family member, or friend. Put an address on the envelope and give the card to the family.

Extensions and Variations:

- Use paper folded in half to make a card if you do not have greeting cards.
- Use stickers to decorate the paper.
- Consider sending a card to a relative who is not well.

HOME CONNECTION

Parents might be willing to save and donate old greeting cards. Ask parents for addresses of family members so you can help the children send the cards. Not every family sends cards for celebrations, so perhaps the child can simply send a note to a family member.

Riding on a Bus

Purpose: Children ride on a pretend bus. They use their imaginations and learn about the bus.

Materials: small chairs
driver's hat

Preparation: 1. Arrange the small chairs in a line to look like seats on a bus.
2. Up to 4 children will enjoy playing at once.

Activity: Pretend to be the bus driver at first. Put on the hat. Sit on the chair at the front of the line and pretend to use a steering wheel. Explain to the children that you are the bus driver and say, "Do you want to ride on the bus? Come in and sit down. We are going for a ride." After a child sits, you might ask, "Julia, do you want to go to the store? This bus goes to the store." Make some engine noises and pretend to drive. Ask the child or children where they want to go. If a child wants to be the bus driver, give her the hat and become a passenger. Continue this activity for as long as the children are interested in playing.

Extensions and Variations:

- Younger children will like just getting in and out of the chairs. Hold the youngest child on your lap so he can play.
- Older children might like to take a stuffed animal or doll with them on the bus.
- Pretend to be on a train or airplane.

HOME CONNECTION

Find out if families use the bus. Ask parents if their child has favorite things about the bus, such as the way the doors open, the bus driver, or the horn. Include this information while playing. Suggest to parents that they play this game at home.

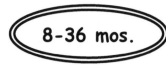

Listening to My Neighborhood

Purpose: While outside on the playground or on a walk, listen to different sounds. Children will learn to identify familiar sounds in this activity.

Materials: none

Preparation: This activity works best with up to 3 children per adult.

Activity: While outside, listen for different sounds. These might include horns, birds, people talking, and vehicles. Ask the child, "What is that sound?" If the child is younger, say "Listen, Josef, that sound is a bird. Can you hear the bird?" When you go back inside, find pictures of the different things you heard making sounds and show these to the children. The pictures help the children connect the sound with an object.

Extensions and Variations:

- Younger children will be especially interested in animal noises and peoples' voices. Loud sudden noises may upset them.
- Older children will be interested in vehicles.

HOME CONNECTION

Ask parents to do this activity as they come to and leave the classroom with their children. They might hear the same sounds and this will help the child become more familiar with neighborhood sounds.

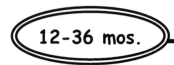

Smells of My Neighborhood

Purpose: Children explore the neighborhood smells outside. They use their sense of smell to understand the neighborhood. This is a great way to learn new words.

Materials: none

Preparation:
1. Go for a walk and explore the types of smells in the neighborhood.
2. This activity can be done while outside on the playground, in a park, or on a walk.
3. Do this with up to 3 children per adult.

Activity: Go outside with the children and observe the different smells. Ask the children to touch their noses and smell. Identify the smell for the younger children. Ask the older children to identify a particular smell. Try to find at least 3 different smells. You might find flowers, leaves, restaurant smells, cigarette smoke, automobile exhaust, or animal smells.

Extensions and Variations:

- Older children enjoy a smell walk. Go on a walk just to smell different things.
- Put different items in bowls or jars in the classroom and see if the children can identify the smells.

HOME CONNECTION

Ask the families if they cook with spices. If they are willing, ask them to bring a small amount of these spices to the school. Arrange up to 3 jars or small bowls of these different spices for the children to smell.

Cooking Applesauce

Purpose: Children help make applesauce and learn about the work of cooks. This activity teaches children where applesauce comes from and how apples change when heated.

Materials: apples
water
sugar
large cooking pot
4 to 5 spoons for stirring
optional: chef's hats or other white hats to wear while cooking

Preparation:
1. Peel and cut the apples for cooking. Save an apple so children can see the whole apple before it is cut.
2. This activity might include up to 4 children and an adult.

Activity: Place the materials on a low table. Invite a few children to make applesauce. Let them explore the whole apple and explain that you have cut other apples to make sauce. Talk with the children about the smell of the apple. The children can help you put the apple pieces in the pot for cooking. If possible, cook the apples in a place where children can watch the cooking. They will enjoy taking a turn stirring while the applesauce cooks. When the apples have turned to mush, bring the mixture to the table for sweetening. Let 1 or 2 children add a small amount of sugar to the applesauce. After the applesauce cools, eat it!

Children enjoy talking about the applesauce they cooked.

Extensions and Variations:

- Spread jam on bread. Older children can learn to use blunt knives and spread the jam by themselves.
- Add chef's hats to the dramatic play area and pretend to make applesauce.
- Take a walk to watch cooks prepare food in a restaurant or school.

HOME CONNECTION

Use the favorite applesauce recipe of family members. Many parents are hesitant to let infants and toddlers cook, but remind them that the children can help in simple ways, such as stirring or pouring ingredients into a bowl. Or, they can play with empty bowls and pans while the parent cooks. If a parent works as a cook, invite her to the classroom to show the children her work clothes.

My Doctor and My Nurse

Purpose: Children examine the tools of health professionals and learn about their work. This activity helps children learn vocabulary used by health professionals and concepts about illness.

Materials:
white shirts for uniforms
play or real stethoscopes
play or real bandages
dolls

Preparation:
1. Assemble the bandages in a small box.
2. Arrange a small area on the rug or in the dramatic play area for this activity.
3. This activity works best with up to 3 children at a time.

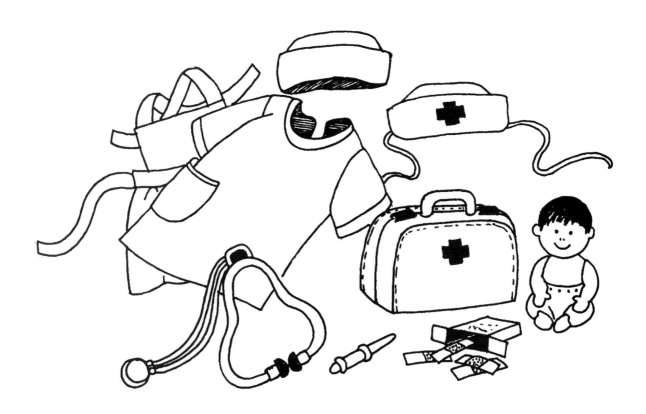

Activity: Explain to the children that the dolls are sick and need care from a doctor or nurse. Invite them to be the doctor or nurse. Put on a "uniform" or shirt and offer one to the child. The child may want to observe first or explore the materials. When the child has done this, ask, "Maria, would you like to see if this baby is sick? Let's use the stethoscope to check the baby's heart. Can you hear it? I think the baby needs a bandage on her leg. Would you like to put the bandage on the baby?"

After coaxing each child to use the materials, the children will start to think of ways to care for the doll themselves. Leave these materials in the classroom for as long as the children are using them. They will go back and repeat the play many times. Add a new material after a while, such as a scale for weighing or tongue depressors, to stimulate more interest. If the group includes very young infants, make sure the materials have large parts that will not cause choking.

Extensions and Variations:

- Invite a nurse or doctor to visit and show the children how to work with the dolls.
- Find pictures of children with a doctor or nurse and put these on display for the children.

HOME CONNECTION

Find out if any family members are nurses or doctors. They might help by donating materials or visiting in their uniforms and talking with the children.

Work Hats

Purpose: Children play with hats of different occupations and learn about work uniforms. Children learn words for different types of work. They also use their imaginations as they pretend to be the workers.

Materials: assorted hats for a chef, policeman, construction worker, street sweeper, or nurse
pictures or book of workers and their hats
mirror
box or basket

Preparation: 1. Place the hats in a box or basket.
2. Try this activity with a small group of 3 children.

Activity: Sit on the floor with the hats around you. Observe the children as they come over and explore the hats. Encourage them to try the hats on. "Josef, would you like to try on the construction worker hat? What a nice hat! You look like a person who builds buildings." Show the children their reflection in the mirror if they are interested. Continue until the children lose interest and go to play elsewhere.

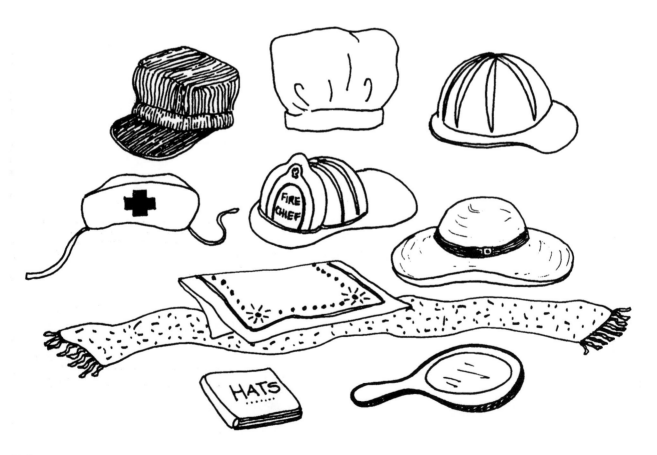

Extensions and Variations:

- Put the hats on hooks or shelves in the dramatic play area for older children.
- Find a book on hats to show younger children. One suggestion is *Hats* by Ann Morris (Mulberry Books, 1989).
- Use everyday hats and hoods instead of work hats.

HOME CONNECTION

Ask family members what types of hats each person wears. Make a list and illustrate it with different hats and display this where children dress. Find out what hats family members wear for work.

REFERENCES

Bronson, M.B. (1995). *The right stuff for children birth to 8.* Washington, DC: NAEYC.

Catlin, C. (1994). *Toddlers together.* Beltsville, MD: Gryphon House.

Deiner, P. (1997). *Infants and toddlers: Development and program planning.* Fort Worth, TX: Harcourt Brace.

Dexter, S. (1995). *Joyful play with toddlers.* Seattle, WA: Parenting Press.

Hast, F. & Hollyfield, A. (1999). *Infant and toddler experiences.* St. Paul, MN: Redleaf Press.

Hawaii Early Learning Profile (HELP). (1988). Vort Corporation.

Herr, J. & Swin, T. (1999). *Creative resources for infants and toddlers.* Albany, NY: Delmar.

Sparrow, S.S., Balla, D.A., & Cicchetti, D.V. (1984). *Vineland Adaptive Behavior Scales.* Circle Pines, MN: American Guidance Service, Inc.

State Education Department, The University of the State of New York. (1996). *How I Grow: Birth Through Five: A Guidebook for Parents.* Albany, NY: Author.

Steelsmith, S. (1995). *Peekaboo and other games to play with your baby.* Seattle, WA: Parenting Press.

Szanton, E.S., editor. (1997). *Creating child-centered programs for infants and toddlers.* Washington, DC: Children's Resources International.

U.S. Consumer Product Safety Commission. (1996). *Which toy for which child? A consumer's guide for selecting suitable toys, ages birth through five.* Washington, DC: author.

Wilmes, C. & Wilmes, D. *2's experience sensory play.* Elgin, IL: Building Blocks.

Developmental Milestones of Children from Birth to Age 3

	Interest in others	Self-awareness	Motor milestones and eye-hand skills
The Early Months (birth through 8 months)	• Newborns prefer the human face and human sound. Within the first 2 weeks, they recognize and prefer the sight, smell, and sound of the principal caregiver. • Social smile and mutual gazing are evidence of early social interaction. Can initiate and terminate these interactions. • Anticipates being lifted or fed and moves body to participate. • Sees adults as objects of interest and novelty. Seeks out adults for play. Stretches arms to be taken.	• Sucks fingers or hand fortuitously. • Observes own hands. • Places hand up as an object comes close to the face as if to protect self. • Looks to the place on body where being touched. • Reaches for and grasps toys. • Clasps hands together and fingers them. • Tries to cause things to happen. • Begins to distinguish friends from strangers. Shows preference for being held by familiar people.	• The young infant uses many complex reflexes: searches for something to suck; holds on when falling; turns head to avoid obstruction of breathing; avoids brightness, strong smells, and pain. • Puts hand or object in mouth. Begins reaching toward interesting objects. • Grasps, releases, regrasps, and releases object again. • Lifts head. Holds head up. Sits up without support. Rolls over. • Transfers and manipulates objects with hands. Crawls.
Crawlers and Walkers (8 to 18 months)	• Exhibits anxious behavior around unfamiliar adults. • Enjoys exploring objects with another as the basis for establishing relationships. • Gets others to do things for child's pleasure (wind up toys, read books, get dolls). • Shows considerable interest in peers. • Demonstrates intense attention to adult language. • Models adult behaviors like vacuuming, setting table, putting on coat and carrying purse to "go work," using a telephone or another object as a telephone. • Enacts simple dramatic play scenarios with others, like caring for dolls, acting like an animal, or riding in a car or train.	• Knows own name. • Smiles or plays with self in mirror. • Uses large and small muscles to explore confidently when a sense of security is offered by presence of caregiver. Frequently checks for caregiver's presence. • Has heightened awareness of opportunities to make things happen, yet limited awareness of responsibility for own actions. • Indicates strong sense of self through assertiveness. Directs actions of others (e.g., "Sit there!") • Identifies one or more body parts. • Begins to use *me, you, I*.	• Sits well in chairs. • Pulls self up, stands holding furniture. • Walks when led. Walks alone. • Throws objects. • Climbs stairs. • Uses marker on paper. • Stoops, trots, can walk backward a few steps.
Toddlers and 2-Year-Olds (18 months to 3 years)	• Shows increased awareness of being seen and evaluated by others. • Sees others as a barrier to immediate gratification. • Begins to realize others have rights and privileges. • Gains greater enjoyment from peer play and joint exploration. • Begins to see benefits of cooperation. • Identifies self with children of same age of sex. • Is more aware of the feelings of others. • Exhibits more impulse control and self-regulation in relation to others. • Enjoys small group activities. • Acts out simple dramatic play themes with others ("You, baby; me, mommy"; going to the store, cooking dinner, preparing for a party.)	• Shows strong sense of self as an individual, as evidenced by "NO" to adult requests. • Experiences self as a powerful, potent, creative doer. Explores everything. • Becomes capable of self-evaluation and has beginning notions of self (good, bad, attractive, ugly). • Makes attempts at self-regulation. • Uses names of self and others. • Identifies 6 or more body parts.	• Scribbles with marker or crayon. • Walks up and down stairs. Can jump off one step. • Kicks a ball. • Stands on one foot. • Threads beads. • Draws a circle. • Stands and walks on tiptoes. • Walks up stairs one foot on each step. • Handles scissors. • Imitates a horizontal crayon stroke.

Language development communication

- Cries to signal pain or distress.
- Smiles or vocalizes to initiate social contact.
- Responds to human voices. In the first month can distinguish familiar human voices from all other sounds. Gazes at faces.
- Uses vocal and nonvocal communication to express interest and exert influence.
- Babbles using all types of sounds. Engages in private conversations when alone.
- Combines babbles. Understands names of familiar people and objects. Laughs. Listens to conversations.
- By about 6 months, distinguishes sounds of home language from other speech.

- Uses eye contact to check back with primary caregiver.
- By about 8 months, turns to look at an object, like a ball, on hearing the word "ball" in the home language.
- Understands many more words than can say. Looks toward 20 or more objects when named.
- Creates long babbled sentences.
- Shakes head no. Says 2 or 3 clear words.
- Looks at picture books with interest, points to objects.
- Uses vocal signals other than crying to gain assistance.
- Begins to use *me, you, I.*

- Combines words.
- Listens to stories for a short while.
- Speaking vocabulary may reach 200 words.
- Develops fantasy in language. Begins to play pretend games.
- Defines use of many household items.
- Uses compound sentences.
- Uses adjectives and adverbs. Recounts events of the day.

Physical, spatial, and temporal awareness

- Comforts self by sucking thumb or finding pacifier.
- Follows a slowly moving object with eyes.
- Recognizes expected patterns of objects in motion (such as arc, bounce, or slide).
- Reaches and grasps toys.
- Looks for dropped toy.
- Remembers intricate details of an object (such as a mobile) and shows signs of recognition on seeing the object again.
- Identifies objects from various viewpoints. Finds a toy hidden under a blanket when placed there while watching.
- Predicts a sequence of events after seeing the sequence a number of times.

- Tries to build with blocks.
- If toy is hidden under 1 of 3 cloths while child watches, looks under the right cloth for the toy.
- Persists in a search for a desired toy even when toy is hidden under distracting objects such as pillows.
- When chasing a ball that rolled under sofa and out the other side, will make a detour around sofa to get ball.
- Pushes foot into shoe, arm into sleeve.

- Identifies a familiar object by touch when placed in a bag with 2 other objects.
- Uses "tomorrow," "yesterday."
- Figures out which child is missing by looking at children who are present.
- Asserts independence: "Me do it."
- Puts on simple garments such as cap or slippers.

Purposeful action and use of tools

- Observes own hands.
- Grasps rattle when hand and rattle are both in view.
- Hits or kicks an object to make a pleasing sight or sound continue.
- Tries to resume a knee ride by bouncing to get adult started again.

- When a toy winds down, continues the activity manually.
- Uses a stick as a tool to obtain a toy.
- When a music box winds down, searches for the key to wind it up again.
- Brings a stool to use for reaching for something.
- Pushes away someone or something not wanted.
- Creeps or walks to get something or avoid unpleasantness.
- Pushes foot into shoe, arm into sleeve.
- Partially feeds self with fingers or spoon.
- Handles cup well with minimal spilling.
- Handles spoon well for self-feeding.

- When playing with a ring-stacking toy, ignores any forms that have no hole. Stacks only rings or other objects with holes.
- Classifies, labels, and sorts objects by group (hard versus soft, large versus small).
- Helps dress and undress self.
- Uses objects as if they were something else (block, as car, big block as bus, box as house).

Expression of feelings

- Expresses discomfort and comfort/pleasure unambiguously.
- Responds with more animation and pleasure to primary caregiver than to others.
- Can usually be comforted by familiar adult when distressed.
- Smiles and shows obvious pleasure in response to social stimulation. Very interested in people. Shows displeasure at loss of social contact.
- Laughs aloud (belly laugh).
- Shows displeasure or disappointment at loss of toy.
- Expresses several clearly differentiated emotions: pleasure, anger, anxiety or fear, sadness, joy, excitement, disappointment, exuberance.
- Reacts to strangers with soberness or anxiety.

- Actively shows affection for familiar person: hugs, smiles at, runs toward, leans against, and so forth.
- Shows anxiety at separation from primary caregiver.
- Shows anger focused on people or objects.
- Expresses negative feelings.
- Shows pride and pleasure in new accomplishments.
- Shows intense feelings for parents.
- Continues to show pleasure in mastery.
- Asserts self, indicating strong sense of self.

- Frequently displays aggressive feelings and behaviors.
- Exhibits contrasting states and mood shifts (stubborn versus compliant).
- Shows increased fearfulness (dark, monsters, etc.).
- Expresses emotions with increasing control.
- Aware of own feelings and those of others.
- Shows pride in creation and production.
- Verbalizes feelings more often. Expresses feelings in symbolic play.
- Shows empathic concern for others.

Source: Lally, J.R., Griffin, A., Fenichel, E., Segal, M., Szanton, E., & Weissbourd, B. (1995). Caring for Infants & Toddlers in Groups: Developmentally Appropriate Practice. Arlington, VA: ZERO TO THREE. Copyright 1995 by ZERO TO THREE. Reprinted with permission.

APPENDIX B

SUGGESTED EQUIPMENT AND FURNITURE
FOR INFANT AND TODDLER CLASSROOMS

Non-Mobile Infants (Birth to 8 Months)

Rugs
Rocking chairs
Adult-size chair
Child-sized chairs (versatile chairs can be bought for play and eating if they have removable trays)
Cribs and bedding
Low toy shelves (2)*
Changing table*
Pillows and mats for crawling or large, foam blocks to make a soft climber
Mirrors (one for the changing table and one to hang low on the wall in the play area)
Strollers
Soft infant swings
CD or cassette player for listening to music

Mobile Infants (8 to 18 Months)

Same as non-mobile infants with the following additions or modifications:

Low table (for up to 6 children) to pull themselves up on and to play on*
Low sensory table for sand and water play*
Low toy shelves (3)*
Small pretend sink, stove, and child-sized cradle for pretend play
Simple blocks*
Push toys with sturdy handles
Low steps and slide with hand rails*
Low wooden, plastic, or foam climber instead of pillows and mats
Soft swings
Tunnel

Toddlers and Two-Year-Olds (18 to 36 months)

Same as non-mobile and mobile infants with the following additions and modifications:

Comfortable adult chair for reading instead of rocking chairs
Low table or tables to seat all of the children
Small cots instead of cribs
Low toy shelves (4 or more to separate play areas)*
Small easel*
Small tricycles and wagons
Low bookshelf*

* Indicates that the item can be made by hand.

APPENDIX C

SUGGESTED PLAY MATERIALS AND TOYS
FOR INFANT AND TODDLER CLASSROOMS

Young Infants (Birth to 8 Months)

Soft balls of different textures (5" diameter)
Small books with 4-5 easy-to-turn pages*
A few light blocks of cloth or rubber (4-6"size)
Soft dolls with painted or molded hair
Lightweight, bright-colored toys for grasping and shaking, such as rattles*
Mobiles*
Bells to shake

Mobile Infants (8 to 18 Months)

Large nontoxic crayons
Rhythm instruments
Large light balls
Cardboard books, simple pictures and stories
Light blocks (approximately 15-25)*
Dolls with faces
Lacing cubes or boards or a few large beads and thick string for lacing*
Hand and finger puppets with simple features, bright colors*
Push and Pull toys with large wheels
Simple puzzles (2-3 pieces) with knobs*
Toy telephone
Funnels and Colanders for sand and water play
Small sand tools (Shovel, bucket)
Simple stacking and nesting toys (3 pieces)*

Toddlers (18 - 24 Months)

Large light balls
Small balls (larger than 1 1/4" diameter)
Light blocks (approximately 20-40)*
Large easy to fit together plastic blocks (e.g., Duplo)
Small people figures (2") to fit in pegboard
Lacing cubes and boards*
Simple rhythm instruments such as bells, drums, and rattles
Simple music box
Peg Boards*
Few small figures (3-5") and animals
Small hand puppets (12")

Push toys with rigid handles
3-5 piece puzzles
Activity boxes*
Simple shape sorters*
Small vehicles (6-8")

Two-Year-Olds

Fingerpaint and tempera paint
Small adjustable easel* with large paper and large blunt brushes
Easy to use blunt scissors
Large balls (10-12" in diameter)
Books that include simple pop-up and hidden pictures, simple stories
Washable dolls (12-15")
Doll clothes with simple fastenings
Dressing frames for buttoning, snapping, lacing, and zipping*
Matching games with 3-5 pairs*
Instruments such as tambourines, sand blocks and simple sound makers
Small people and animals
4-5 piece puzzles
Pots and pans with covers for pretend play
Dress-up clothes
Boats for water play
Simple sieves and strainers, and water wheels for water play
Small toy vehicles (3-4")
Large trucks for block play
Large sand tools

* Indicates that the item can be made by hand.

APPENDIX D

CHECKLIST FOR SELECTING PLAY MATERIALS AND TOYS FOR INFANT AND TODDLER CLASSROOMS

IS THE TOY SAFE?   *YES*   *NO*

—Is it durable?

—Is it breakable?

—Is it too large to be swallowed?

—Does it have sharp edges?

—Does it have small, removable pieces?

—Could the toy pinch the child's fingers or skin?

—Is it made of non-toxic materials?

—Is it made of non-flammable fabric?

DOES THE TOY PROMOTE DEVELOPMENT?

—Does it use the child's senses?

—Does the toy involve the child in an active manner?

—Is the toy appropriate for the child's age?

—Does the toy use multiple developmental skills?

—Is the toy appropriate for helping a child understand
     different cultures and races?

—Does the toy complement other materials in the classroom?

APPENDIX E

SAMPLE DEVELOPMENTAL GOALS CHART FOR INFANTS AND TODDLERS

Daily Routines	Non-Mobile Infants	Mobile Infants	Toddlers
Arrival	* smiles * reaches * responds to voices * coos/babbles	* waves "hello" * vocalizes * begins to take off outer clothes	* says "hello" * walks carrying bag * takes off outer clothes * hangs up bag in cubby
Feeding	* cries/fusses to indicate hunger * makes eye contact * smiles, vocalizes * turns toward voices and sounds * reaches/holds the bottle	* points/gestures * holds a bottle or cup * eats crackers, finger foods * begins to use utensils to eat	* communicates hunger verbally * climbs into chair * eats independently * uses thumb & forefinger to pick up small objects * indicates "more" * labels food items * washes & dries hands
Diapering/Toileting	* cries/fusses to indicate discomfort * makes eye contact * smiles, vocalizes * imitates sounds * may roll over or kick legs * grasps objects	* cries/fusses to indicate discomfort * points/gestures to indicate need * helps by holding bottom up and putting feet into pants legs * responds to directions	* may verbalize need to be changed to go to the bathroom * initiates toileting * unfastens clothing * stays dry longer * washes and dries hands *acknowledges going to the bathroom
Dressing	* coos/babbles * plays 'peekaboo' * begins to bend arms and legs to cooperate * looks at self in mirror * looks for dropped objects	* initiates own dressing games * removes small clothing items * assists in putting on clothes and moving arms and legs	* dresses in simple, large clothes * names clothing, common objects * opinionated on fabrics, colors, items * removes clothing with little or no assistance * shows body parts * follows two simple directions

Daily Routines	Young Infants	Mobile Infants	Toddlers
Napping/Sleeping	* cries/fusses when tired or alert * rolls over * recognizes familiar faces and objects when waking * anticipates returns	* going-to-sleep ritual lengthens * cries/fusses when tired * points/gestures to crib or sleep area	* points/gestures when tired * verbalizes desire or need to sleep * may resist sleep * helps with tasks (puts blankets away)
Private Play	*observes own hands and feet * reaches for and grasps toys * sits with support * transfers toys from hand to hand * sucks hands and fingers	* smiles at or plays with self in mirror * gets into sitting * explores environment, objects * crawls, cruises, walks with support * scribbles * turns pages of book * seeks out preferred toys	* plays pretend games * explores surroundings * plays alone * shows affection to dolls, people * colors, paints * jumps * takes things apart and puts them together * names pictures in book
Peer Play	* coos/babbles * shows dislike when familiar toy is removed * makes eye contact	* explores objects with others * shows interest in peers * initiates social games like ball	* listens to stories, rhymes, music * completes simple puzzles * plays pretend games, role plays * throws ball with aim
Departure	* may greet parent happily or be matter-of-fact * smiles back at adults * recognizes parent * controls head when carried	* may be absorbed in activity and resist leaving * may resent parent for leaving and ignore or resist * uses words like mama and bye-bye * waves, vocalizes good-bye	* answers questions * can pick up and put away activity * may protest leaving activity * answers simple questions * uses personal pronouns

Source: Martha L. Venn and Juliann Woods Cripe, *Creating Child-Centered Programs for Infants and Toddlers*, Washington, DC: Children's Resources International, p. 114.

CREATING CHILD-CENTERED CLASSROOM SERIES

CREATING CHILD-CENTERED CLASSROOMS: 3-5 YEAR OLDS

Helps teachers create active learning environments for preschool-age children, individualize teaching, and involve families in the program. Teachers learn observation techniques to teach to the strengths, interests, and needs of each child.

CREATING CHILD-CENTERED MATERIALS FOR MATH AND SCIENCE

Assists educators in designing and making their own classroom materials for active exploration in math and science. Each activity includes a "home connection" that links the child's family to the classroom learning experiences. Easy-to-follow directions allow teachers to create activities from recycled and natural materials.

CREATING CHILD-CENTERED CLASSROOMS: 6-7 YEAR OLDS

Provides teachers with lessons, suggestions for extending activities, assessment strategies and forms, thematic curriculum webs, and complete resource and reference lists. This volume presents four powerful themes that unify program concepts and goals: Communication, Caring, Community, and Connections.

CREATING CHILD-CENTERED PROGRAMS FOR INFANTS AND TODDLERS

Provides the research base that supports the need for quality programs. It shows caregivers how to design a safe, healthy, and responsive environment for infants and toddlers; how to support young children's learning; and how to staff and evaluate a child-centered program for infants and toddlers.

LEARNING ACTIVITIES FOR INFANTS AND TODDLERS: AN EASY GUIDE FOR EVERYDAY USE

Offers caregivers more than 100 hands-on, developmentally appropriate activities that caregivers can incorporate into the child's day. Each activity includes a purpose, list of materials, and simple steps for preparation. In addition, each activity provides a "home connection," to involve parents and extend the activity at home.

CREATING INCLUSIVE CLASSROOMS

Provides the research base, practical methods and real-world case studies that guide and support teachers through issues such as family partnerships, IEP development, and adapting the classroom environment.

CREATING CHILD-CENTERED CLASSROOMS: 8-10 YEAR OLDS

Presents a unique blend of current, exemplary educational practices and sound theory to address the educational needs of children in the later early childhood years. It addresses the content areas of mathematics, literacy, social studies, science, and the visual arts.

For more information, contact:

Children's Resources International
5039 Connecticut Ave., NW
Suite One
Washington, DC 20008
phone: 202-363-9002
fax: 202-363-9550
info@crinter.com

EDUCATION AND THE CULTURE OF DEMOCRACY

Explains the link between democracy and early childhood practice. This book contends that there are subtle, yet effective teaching techniques that encourage democracy: choice, individualism, creativity, equality, respect for differences, and appreciation of individuals' needs while maintaining the balance for the greater good of the group.